Divine Impact

Divine Impact

25 Bible Passages That Can Enrich Our Lives

by
Paul Sullivan Pope

Crestwick Books
San Antonio, Texas

Published by Crestwick Books
An Imprint of Visions Audio Publishing, Inc.
9200 Powhatan
San Antonio, Texas 78230

Printed in the United States of America

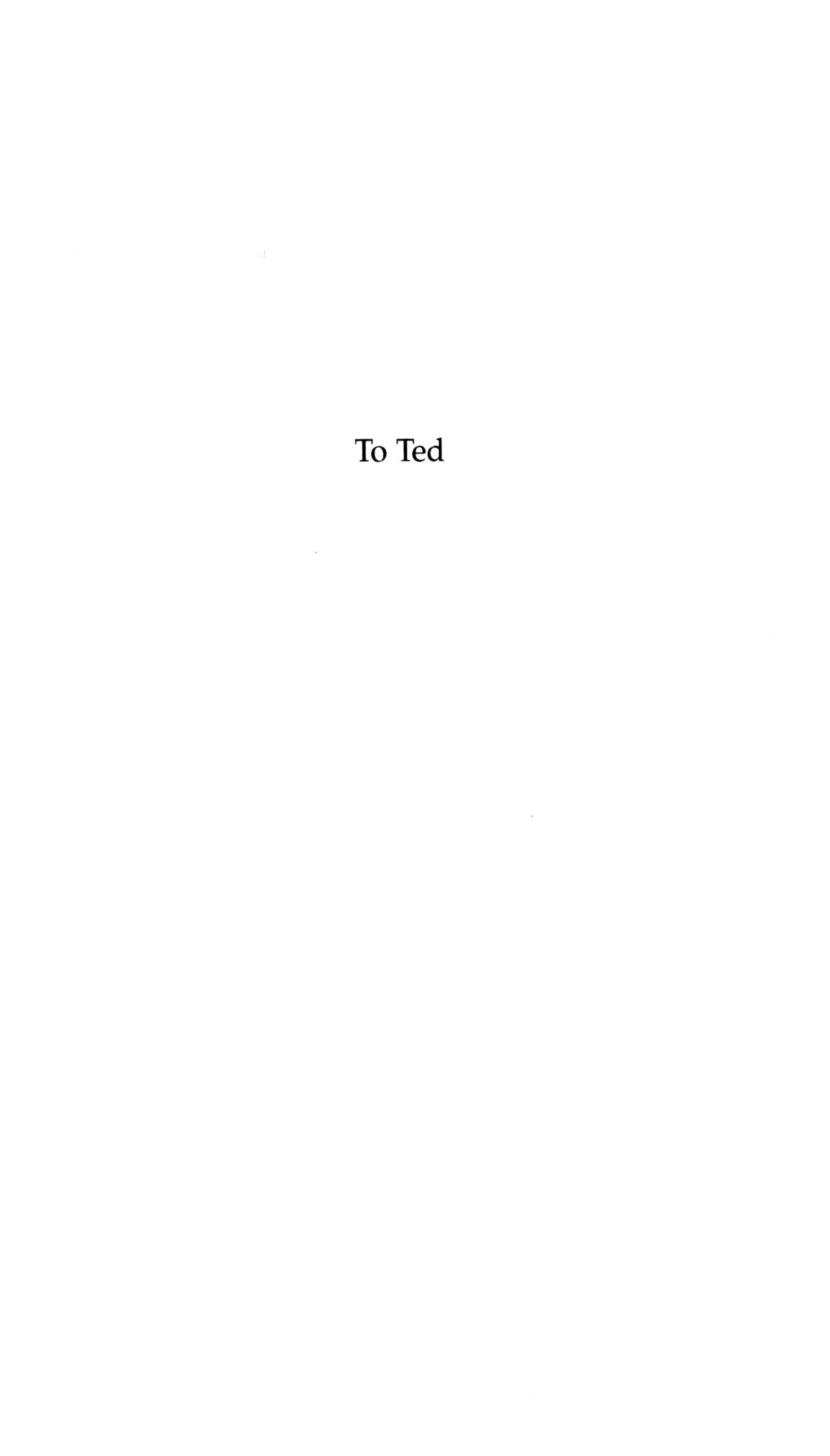

To Ted

Contents

Contents

Contents

Acknowledgements

This book could not have been completed without the help of members of my family who supported this effort with tolerance, patience and honest criticism. I especially appreciate my wife Joan and my daughters Linda Parker and Sharon Byler. They all contributed significantly to the timely completion of the manuscript.

Design and composition was performed by my old friend Gene Cuthbertson of No. 9 Graphics in San Antonio.   He too exhibited patience, especially with my slow and deliberate reading of galley proofs.

I am also grateful for the work of SeSee Munson at Grunwald Printing in Corpus Christi. She and her colleagues did the necessary pre-production work to prepare the manuscript for printing.

My special thanks go to Warren Spanutius, who gave me moral and material support, and whose encouragement was invaluable.

Preface

For centuries the Inspired Word of God as expressed in the Holy Bible has been changing lives. Such changes sometimes take the form of sudden conversions similar to the experience of the Apostle Paul on the Road to Damascus. But in many cases reading the Bible changes lives in less dramatic ways. My own experience has taken the latter course as I slowly developed an understanding of what life-changing power the Word of God contains.

Over a period of years as I read, reread and studied the Bible, sometimes under the guidance of erudite leaders, other times by following study guides, and still other times going it alone, I gradually came to know just how important this Book of books is. With each succeeding investigation of Scripture and with every discussion with others of like interest, I was thrust into further study. I found myself increasingly absorbed and was always compelled to continue, to keep on reading and studying, to keep on searching for what God has to say—not only to all humankind, but also to me as an individual.

After being profoundly affected by what I read in the Bible, I have come to the conclusion that this collection of writings truly is inspired by God. The Bible has had a "divine impact" on millions of readers throughout the ages, yet people who have experienced the positive power of the Bible describe the effect on their lives in different ways. Learning of God's love for us and discovering His desire to save us from our sins are paramount. But there is much, much more to this amazing Book. I have been particularly taken by the Bible's wise counsel regarding how we might conduct our lives in ways that satisfy our souls and which foster harmony among us. I consider this collective wisdom as "life-enriching." And such wise counsel is not confined to the so-called wisdom books—Proverbs, Job and Ecclesiastes—but may be gleaned from all parts of the Bible.

The Bible contains more life-enriching inspiration than can be covered in this one small volume. For this book I have selected 25 especially inspirational and meaningful passages from the many wonderful choices. They are organized along topical lines and placed in numbered chapters, with brief introductory comments explaining why each passage was included. Following each passage is a commentary that relates my impression of how that Scripture has relevance to life in the 21st century—how that particular writing can enrich our lives and change the way we view the world. Finally, each chapter concludes with an easy-to remember *Life Enrichment Axiom* that assists readers in applying the principal lesson of the passage to real life.

The passages quoted are from a modernized version of the King James Bible, modified only in terms of updating verb and pronoun forms, and exchanging the occasional archaic word to equivalent modern terminology. Meanings have not been altered in any way.

Author's note: Readers should know that the author is neither a trained theologian nor an ordained minister. Rather, I am a writer, teacher and sometimes television producer and script consultant. I have written this book, and selected the Bible passages that make up the heart of it, based on the impact they have had on my life. Of course, I have been influenced by reading the works of other writers who have studied the Bible more than I have, but my primary resource has been the Bible itself.

The commentaries which follow the passages are my own reflections on how reading those passages have affected me. The same passages may mean different things to you, depending on your own background, life experiences and ideas. There are certainly differences of opinion held by Bible scholars of what much of the Bible means. So I wish to make it

clear that my commentaries are strictly my own
impressions of how God has spoken to me through
His word. It is perfectly valid for you to have different impressions.

Paul Sullivan Pope
November, 2003

Introduction

*As you read the Bible you should constant-
ly affirm that Divine Wisdom is enlight-
ening you. That is the way to get direct
inspiration.*

—Emmett Fox

The first two chapters of this book concern passages from the first part of the Book of
Genesis. The Creation and the Fall may not be
considered life-enriching by some readers, but they
establish certain assumptions upon which the passages that follow them rely. After reading the passages and the commentaries which follow them, you
can then proceed through the rest of the book, recognizing what assumptions imbue the whole work.

As you read, keep in mind that inspirational works
are not limited to those that provide encouragement
or warm the heart. There are those, but also included
are passages that have the power to singe our minds
and perhaps awaken us out of apathy or thoughtless
routines. Other selected passages inspire us to think
more deeply about mankind's relationship to the
Creator than we might have done before. Still others
may point us in an entirely new spiritual direction.
Whatever inspiration you find in these writings, read-

ing from the Holy Bible can't help but enrich your life.

So, we begin. And what better place than at the beginning.

To understand life is to try to understand God, to understand what he intends, where he intends to lead us by means of events, by means of our successes and our failures. The value, the infinite value, of the biblical perspective is that it radically changes our attitude in the face of the events of life.

—Paul Tournier

1

The Beginning of All Things
The Story of Creation from the Book of Genesis

Whether the reader believes in the literalness of the first Chapter of Genesis matters not if he or she accepts God as the force behind it all. Some believe God created the universe and all that is within it in six earthly days. Others believe He created all things, but chose as His method an evolutionary process covering millions of years. This is not the place for such discourse. Suffice it to say that gaining inspiration from the first chapter of Genesis requires only that the reader believe that God *did* create all things. We need not know how He did it. There are many mysteries in the Bible, and even with all our scientific knowledge and study of scriptures, we will perhaps never in this life know the answers to those mysteries. If we did, would we need faith? As you read this passage, consider the awesome power of the One who created all things.

Divine Impact

Genesis: Chapter 1, Verse 1, through Chapter 2, Verse 3

In the beginning God created the heaven and the earth. And the earth was without form, and void; and darkness was upon the face of the deep. And the Spirit of God moved upon the face of the waters.

And God said, "Let there be light," and there was light. And God saw the light, that it was good, and God divided the light from the darkness. And God called the light Day, and the darkness he called Night. And the evening and the morning were the first day.

And God said, "Let there be a firmament in the midst of the waters, and let it divide the waters from the waters." And God made the firmament, and divided the waters which were under the firmament from the waters which were above the firmament, and it was so. And God called the firmament Heaven. And the evening and the morning were the second day.

And God said let the waters under the heaven be gathered together in one place, and let the dry land appear, and it was so. And God called the dry land Earth, and the gathering together of the waters he called Seas; and God saw that it was good.

The Beginning of All Things

And God said, "Let the earth bring forth grass, the herb yielding seed, and the fruit tree yielding fruit, after their kind, with seed in them, upon the earth." And it was so.

And the earth brought forth grass, and herb yielding seed after their kind, and the tree yielding fruit with seed in it, after its kind; and God saw that it was good. And the evening and the morning were the third day.

And God said, "Let there be lights in the firmament of the heaven to divide the day from the night; and let them be for signs, and for seasons, and for days, and years. And let them be for lights in the firmament of the heaven to give light upon the earth." And it was so. And God made two great lights, the greater light to rule the day, and the lesser light to rule the night. He made the stars also. And God set them in the firmament of the heaven to give light upon the earth, and to rule over the day and over the night, and to divide the light from the darkness. And God saw that it was good. And the evening and the morning were the fourth day.

And God said, "Let the waters bring forth abundantly the moving creature that has life, and fowl that may fly above the earth in the open firmament of heaven." And God created great whales, and every living creature that moves, which the waters brought forth abundantly, after their kind, and every winged fowl after its kind. And God saw that it was good. And God blessed them and told them to be fruitful, and multiply, and fill the waters in the seas, and let fowl multiply in the earth. And the evening and the morning were the fifth day.

And God said, "Let the earth bring forth the living creature after its kind: cattle, creeping thing, and beast of the earth after their kind." And it was so. And God made the beast of the earth after its kind, and cattle after its kind, and every thing that creeps upon the earth after its kind. And God saw that it was good.

And God said, "Let us make man in our image, after our likeness; and let them have dominion over the fish of the sea, and over the fowl of the air, and over the cattle, and over all the earth, and over every creeping thing that creeps upon the earth." So God created man in his own image; in the image of God he made them—male and female.

And God blessed them, and God told them to be fruitful and multiply, and replenish the earth, and subdue it, and have dominion over the fish of the sea, and over the fowl of the air, and over every living thing that moves upon the earth.

And God said, "Look, I have given you every

The Beginning of All Things

herb-bearing seed, which is on the face of all the earth, and every tree, in the which is the fruit of a tree yielding seed; so that you will have food to eat. And to every beast of the earth, and to every fowl of the air, and to every thing that creeps upon the earth, wherein there is life, I have given every green herb for food." And it was so.

And God saw everything that he had made, and, it was very good. And the evening and the morning were the sixth day. Thus the heavens and the earth were finished.

And on the seventh day God ended his work which he had made; and he rested on the seventh day from all the work he had done. And God blessed the seventh day, and sanctified it, because it was the day he had rested from all the work of creation.

Inspired by God's Power

If you have ever been away from city lights on a clear night and looked up at the stars, you know what an awesome sight it is. If you are not immediately impressed, and I cannot imagine your not being, just start counting the stars and see how far you get. If you are patient and persistent and keep counting until the stars disappear at dawn, you will find that you haven't covered much of the sky. And if you have a wide angle view of the sky through a powerful telescope on the same kind of clear night and could somehow mark your spot in the sky and continue counting the next night and the next and the next, you would never finish counting, even if you lived to be a hundred.

Astronomers do not know how many stars there are because they can't see beyond where the limits our most powerful telescopes take us. To use a common phrase in its truest sense, "God knows" how many stars there are—first because He is omniscient, but also because He made them. Not only did He make them, but He made them out of nothing, just as He created everything else out of nothing.

Think a moment of the complexity of the structure of matter. God had to design the whole thing—molecules, atoms, protons, electrons, neutrons, quarks and whatever else might lie even deeper into the structure of matter than those. Then He developed a system to control how all the pieces would work together—the laws of nature. That's for starters. Then on one planet orbiting one of the stars God organized some of the matter in such a way that it came alive—the seemingly infinite variety of living things.

Of all the living things God created and placed on planet earth the most complex by far is the human. God gave these animals something extra. He gave them a spiritual dimension and a capacity for reasoning and creating, then put them in charge of the whole planet.

The story of creation speaks to the magnitude of God—how big and how great He is. Some people, however, believe there is no God, and that all things came into being by some inexplicable means. Here's a theory many of them subscribe to: Matter always existed, bound up in one big ball that in time exploded and sent everything flying through space, forming numerous galaxies far, far into the distance. And in one of those galaxies some of the matter organized itself into nine planets orbiting one small star in that galaxy—and possibly into many more planets orbiting many other stars. This was accomplished with no pre-planning or design—just a curious accident.

The only flaw in that theory is not that a big bang couldn't have happened to give form to matter, but how did the matter get there in the first place? Who made the matter? Who knew how to make it explode at exactly the right time to create the universe? Who initiated the idea of gravity and the other laws that govern the way matter behaves?

Here is another theory: Some Super Being whose power is unfathomable to us humans had to have pre-existed the formation of the universe and all of its components. This theory holds that a Super Being had to have made matter itself.

The concept of any being, super or otherwise, which pre-existed matter makes my head hurt, but much less so than the theory that matter always existed. God may indeed have used something like the big bang to create the universe, but if He did it was His method of choice and not happenstance. That is what I believe.

How and out of what material God created the universe are questions humankind has explored and debated throughout recorded history, and probably long before that. Whatever the answers to those questions are, God did some pretty awesome work.

The story of Creation may not be everyone's idea of inspiration. But when you consider the big picture, this passage has got to rank right up near the top; for without a beginning, there could be no middle, in which we now exist, nor could there be an end, where the material world and all that is in it is headed.

Again, whether or not all things were brought into existence in six literal days is not the important point here. The message is that a Supreme Being, whom we call God, made all that there is: all matter, all laws of nature, and all life—plants, animals, humans and any alien creatures that may exist out there somewhere.

A God who can create a star, much less untold numbers of galaxies of them; a God who can arrange the heavenly bodies so as to provide all that sustains life on this small planet; a God who can create a minia-

Divine Impact

ture rose and a mighty oak tree, a babbling brook and a vast ocean, an apple and a pumpkin, a kitten and a rhinoceros, a guppy and a whale, a hummingbird and an eagle; and a God who can create a baby with the potential to grow to maturity and change the world, is indeed inspiring.

What a demonstration of power! Simply awesome! Before proceeding to the other twenty four passages contained in this book, it seemed appropriate to ponder the awesome power of God. Recognition of that limitless power is the basis for adopting a world view that has God at the center, which, in turn, can help readers discover in the remaining passages the ways in which their lives may be enriched. Novelist Morris West put it this way:

> *Once you accept the existence of God—however you define him, however you explain your relationship to him—you are caught forever with his presence at the center of all things.*

The Beginning of All Things

Life Enrichment Axiom 1:

When we realize the awesome power of God as expressed in His creation, we have taken the first step in allowing Him to reside in the core of our being.   And with Him as our center, we are open to His desire to enrich our lives.

2

---

*When we have understood free will we shall see how
silly it is to ask, as somebody once asked me, "Why did God
make a creature of such rotten stuff that it went wrong?"*
—C. S. Lewis

Adam And Eve: The First Screw-ups

The Story of the Fall, from the Book of Genesis

How, you may wonder, can we find anything inspirational in the story of humankind's fall from God's grace? Well, I admit it's not easy. But in telling the story of Adam and Eve's big no-no, disobeying God, the writer of Genesis reminds us of something very dear to us: that humans have choices. The story of Adam and Eve in the garden simply tells us about the first time we exercised that privilege.

Adam and Eve

When the serpent tempted Eve he knew she had free will, otherwise she couldn't be tempted to eat the forbidden fruit. So God had obviously built free will into humans at the very beginning. God apparently was willing to take the risk that we would screw up now and again. But I can imagine that He could not see much purpose in making us a bunch of robots while He sat in heaven acting as a giant main-frame computer controlling our every action. Without choice, without right and wrong, where would the drama of life be? Without an option to hate, what is the value of love? Without suffering, how can anyone have compassion? Without the threat of danger, where is the need for courage?

When God gave us free will He established a basic value system for us. The system is a simple one, composed of only two choices: Obey God, or do what you please. With their original act of disobedience, Adam and Eve started what people through the succeeding millennia have continued to do.

J. B. Phillips, Anglican priest, author and New Testament translator, explains what all that disobedience has led to:

Divine Impact

The cumulative effect over the centuries of millions of individuals choosing to please themselves rather than the Designer of the "whole show" has infected the whole planet. This is what theologians mean when they call this a sinful world.

As you read the third chapter of Genesis and bemoan the fact that Adam and Eve made a bad choice, consider their not having the choice. Consider a world of smiling robots and valueless daily routines. Recognize that God in his wisdom and love for us gave us that most precious of freedoms—free will, and with it, the opportunity to prove our mettle.

Adam and Eve

Genesis: Chapter Three, Verses 1 through 19

Now the serpent was more subtle than any beast of the field which the Lord God had made. And he said to the woman, "Did God say that you shall not eat of every tree of the garden?" And the woman said to the serpent, "We may eat of the fruit of the trees of the garden, but of the fruit of the tree which is in the midst of the garden, God said 'You shall not eat of it, neither shall you touch it, or you shall die.'" And the serpent said to the woman, "You shall not surely die, for God knows that on the day you eat the fruit of that tree your eyes shall be opened, and you shall be as gods, knowing good and evil."

And when the woman saw that the tree was good for food, and that it was pleasant to the eyes, and a tree to be desired to make one wise, she took of the fruit thereof, and ate it, and also gave it to her husband, who ate it, too. And the eyes of them both were opened, and they knew that they were naked; and they sewed fig leaves together, and made themselves aprons. And they heard the voice of the LORD God walking in the garden in the cool of the day; and Adam and his wife hid themselves from the presence of the LORD God among the trees of the garden.

Divine Impact

And the LORD God called unto Adam, and said unto him, "Where are you?" And Adam said, "I heard your voice in the garden, and I was afraid, because I was naked; and I hid myself."

And he said, "Who told you that you were naked? Have you eaten of the tree, whereof I commanded you that you should not eat?" And the man said, "The woman you gave to me gave me the fruit of the tree and I ate it." And the LORD God said unto the woman, "What have you done?" And the woman said, "The serpent beguiled me, and I ate it."

And the LORD God said to the serpent, "Because you have done this, you are cursed above all cattle, and above every beast of the field; upon your belly shall you go, and dust shall you eat all the days of your life. And I will put enmity between you and the woman, and between your seed and her seed. It shall bruise your head, and you shall bruise his heel."

To the woman he said, "I will greatly multiply your sorrow and your conception; in sorrow you shall bring forth children; and your desire shall be to your husband, and he shall rule over you."

And to Adam he said, "Because you have listened to the voice of your wife, and have eaten of the tree of which I commanded you, saying, 'You shall not eat of it,' cursed is the ground for your sake. In sorrow shall you eat of it all the days of your life. Thorns also and thistles shall it bring forth to you, and you shall eat the herb of the field. In the sweat of your face shall you eat bread, until you return to the ground; for out of it were you taken: for you are dust, and unto dust you shall return."

Divine Impact

The Spice of Life

Once in a religion class, when someone asked the teacher why God created people, we got the best explanation I ever heard. I, like most of my classmates, was in my late twenties—still "searching for the truth," as young thinking people like to say. After the question was asked, the older, wiser teacher answered with a parable, as Jesus might have done if the question were posed to Him. The parable likened a new recording of beautiful music to God's creation. The story that follows is loosely based on that parable—expanded, altered and embellished for the sake of clarity, as I do not have the benefit of interaction with my readers as the teacher did with his students. But this, I believe, gets the point across:

Before anything existed outside of heaven, God stood on his heavenly podium conducting his orchestra and chorus of angels as they played the most beautiful music imaginable. When the music was over, he thought, "Wow, that is truly beautiful! I really love it! I want to share this with somebody." So he made a CD of it and labeled it "Creation." Then he thought, "But who can I share it with? There isn't anybody. The angels don't count because they'll go along with anything I say." Then he got this brilliant idea. "I know, I'll create somebody to share it with, somebody who will love it like I do." So he took one of the notes from his score and made a man with it. Then he took a part of the man and made a woman.

When he had completed making the man and the woman, and was ready to play the CD for them, he realized that there was something missing. "If I play this music for them they will have to love it like I do and like the angels do because they are like little me's. What value is it if they like it just because I do and not of their own free will? I guess I will have to give them a choice—the freedom to not like it." So he came up with the idea to build freedom of choice into his new creatures, thinking that, "Even though now they have the choice of rejecting the music, they will surely like it because it is so beautiful."

Lucifer, one of the angels in God's choir, heard all this and went to God with a question. "If those new creatures have free will, why can't we?" God answered, "You've always had it but you didn't need to use it because you saw truth and beauty all around you every day." Lucifer replied, "Yes, I know, but you used your free will when you put me in the back row of the choir. Why can't I be a soloist? And by the way, I believe that I could compose music, too, if you'd let me."

God told the angel that the choir was arranged so as to make the music perfect, and he wouldn't change it.

Lucifer got very upset, and said, "Well, if that's the way it's going to be, I'd rather go someplace else."

God asked him, "Where else do you think there is to go?"

Lucifer thought about it a moment and said, "I don't know."

God then said, "Well, I don't want you around here messing with all the contented angels, so I'll tell you what I'm going to do. There's a new position open on the planet earth. That new species I put there have many of my own traits, but on a much reduced scale. I have given them free will so that they will have the choice to love or to reject my music. It isn't fair for humans to have free will but not have any real options, so you go down there and play your own music for them. Give them a choice. I doubt if your music will be anywhere near as good as mine, but if you want to do your own thing, have at it."

Lucifer said, "I'm ready; send me

now." God answered, "There's one thing you need to know. Once you leave, you can't come back."

"Don't worry," the angel said, "I won't want to. I've had it with all this goody, goody stuff. Adios."

So God put the CD on and started playing it so that when the humans awoke to begin living they would hear it. Then he released the disgruntled Lucifer to go down to earth to try to distract humans with his own kind of music, although God hoped they would never listen to any music but his own.

When Lucifer, who as a spirit had no form, got to earth, where God had placed the humans, he needed visibility. So he entered a snake and slithered over to a spot near where the humans were.

Now God spoke to the humans and told them, "Just listen to my beautiful music! Isn't it marvelous? I want you to relax and enjoy it, and you will if you don't let anything distract you. Just focus on your appreciation for truth and beauty that I have instilled in you. Above all, don't forget who played it for you. Okay? Now listen ."

So God played his music for the new creatures, and at first they liked it. Then they were distracted by another voice, not God's, calling them to come listen to some other music. The woman heard the voice first and went to check it out. She saw a snake and followed it until she came across a CD player with a CD labeled "Do It Your Way" playing. It sounded pretty good to her, so she brought it back to the man and played it for him.

But when it was mixed with God's music everything sounded discordant. God didn't like the competition, but he kept on playing his music, hoping that the humans would turn off the other CD and listen to his only. It was far superior to what Lucifer had composed and sung for them, but they liked to think they could do whatever they wanted. God asked the humans why they played it, and what it was that had distracted them from his music. The man and the woman were embarrassed, but laid all the blame on the snake. God then said to them,

"I told you to listen to the music I was playing for you and not let yourself be distracted. But you've gone and done it now. So you'll just have to live with your choice and listen to all kinds of music from now on. And I'm warning you: some of it can get pretty bad."

And it was so.

As allegory this simple little story can't be held up to strict scrutiny, but it does illustrate two things. One, we must have free will, otherwise nothing has value. And two, we are going to be disobedient at times, maybe even most of the time, but it's up to us.

Adam and Eve

Make the wrong choice and the consequences can be hurtful, either to ourselves or to others or both. Make the correct choice and there's a much greater chance that life's troubles will be fewer.

Unfortunately, making correct choices does not assure us of an easy or successful problem-free life. A major obstacle to finding Heaven on earth is the way humans interact with other humans. All too often we make choices of what to do or what to say that hurt others, sometimes in horrible ways. Another difficulty is that sometimes it's hard to know which choice is the right one. Most of us want to make the right choices, but sometimes we don't know what they are.

Fortunately, God has provided us with a handbook. It's called the Holy Bible, and it is full of lessons on how to make the best choices, and on how to deal with the hurts that can come to any of us by the wrong choices we or others might make. Some of those lessons are revealed in this collection of passages.

We must be careful here so as not to fall for the same trick Adam and Eve did when they accepted Lucifer's deception that they could be like God and

Divine Impact

decide for themselves what was good and what was evil. The Bible is not a replacement for God, not a formula for always doing the right thing. God wants to be involved in our lives. We need God's written word, to be sure, but we must also maintain regular contact with the Author Himself. The Bible in our lives is sort of like a football player's playbook. There is plenty to learn in it, but it takes a coach to show all the players how to work with other team members to execute the plays. And just as a coach works all season long to keep his team performing at a high level, we need God to work with us all our lives. I like Paul Tournier's plain and simple way of defining the problem:

> *The fatal error of men is this very aspiration to be like God, knowing good and evil, wanting to have a moral code so as to be able to act on their own without any further need of God to enlighten them step by step.*

Can we be inspired by the story of the fall of humankind? Yes, if we recognize that it happened because we misused our free will. But free will is one of God's greatest gifts, the basis for all that makes life an adventure. Without it we would forfeit all opportunities to express love, virtue and creativity. And it is inspiring to realize that despite the bad choice Adam and Eve made and the bad choices all of us continue to make, God loves us and believes in us so much that he is willing to keep on giving us opportunities to make the right choices. He also promises to be available to help us make those choices. The catch is we must remember to ask Him, then listen to His answers.

Life Enrichment Axiom 2:

Recognizing that God gave us freedom of choice to establish our value system, we know that by choosing to seek God's guidance we will make better, life-enriching decisions.

3

Joshua—A Man with a Purpose

Choosing Sides in the Game of Life

From the story of humankind's first bad choice we move to a very short passage that reflects a correct choice. It is recorded in the book of Joshua and is from the words of Joshua himself, the successor to Moses as leader of the exodus of the Jews from Egypt. It is a simple statement that clearly reveals Joshua's understanding and acceptance of God's supremacy. But the simplicity of Joshua's statement cannot detract from it's importance. It is the

Joshua—A Man With a Purpose

hallmark of faith. That is why it is so inspiring.
Joshua's words are simple, clear, and yet profound.

Divine Impact

Joshua: Chapter 24, Verse 15

"...choose you this day whom you will serve...but
as for me and my house, we will serve the LORD."

Joshua—A Man With a Purpose

Commitment: The Foundation of Character

In this passage, Joshua essentially said to his comrades, "You guys can do whatever you want to, but I'm going to serve the Lord." No two ways about it. Joshua was committed. That kind of certainty, that kind of commitment to serve an earthly cause, is admirable in most any situation, but when it reflects one's commitment to God's cause it is downright inspiring. This guy Joshua didn't have to mull it over or discuss it with a friend or a family member. He knew what he was going to do. No shillyshallying, no argument, no question—he was committed.

If you are in a position of responsibility—a manager of a business, a military officer, a line supervisor, a teacher, or even a parent—wouldn't you want all those under your authority to have that all-out commitment? I believe anyone would. Much can be accomplished by a team of people with such unwavering allegiance to their cause. Imagine what kind of a world we would have if everyone made a pledge to commit to doing their very best in all their relationships. And consider how the world would change if everyone made the same commitment to serve God that Joshua did.

Life Enrichment Axiom 3:

We are ready to enter into an important relationship only when we are willing to make a commitment to give it our all and stay the course.

4

Home is where the heart is.
                        —Anonymous

A Foreign Woman Finds Her True Home

The Family Loyalty of Ruth

Loyalty is the second stage of commitment— the follow through. Once a commitment is made and the sometimes difficult work of carrying out the mutually agreed upon task or mission is set in motion, loyalty develops as the natural consequence. This premise assumes that both parties involved have made equally strong commitments.

Divine Impact

With serious commitments becoming more and more an endangered species, loyalty is becoming an increasingly rare virtue. Sometimes when it is displayed it seems truly remarkable. Friends who stand by you when it might mean they will be required to bear all or part of your burden are friends indeed. Family members who go to bat for each other when difficulties arise strengthen the whole family unit. Athletes who play for a losing team without their eyes constantly on the lookout for opportunities to play for a better team inspire their teammates and help them rise to a higher level of achievement. Too bad these demonstrations of loyalty are less common than they once were, although the loyalty to fallen comrades displayed by rescue workers at the site of the World Trade Center tragedy is a hopeful sign that the trend may be reversing.

As we will see in the following reading, Ruth, a Moabite woman, had an undying loyalty to her mother-in-law, Naomi, who was an Israelite. It turned out to be a blessing for Ruth as well as for Naomi, as it often does for anyone who has that rare quality—loyalty.

The Family Loyalty of Ruth

The Book of Ruth:
Chapter 1, Verses 1 through 18

Now it came to pass in the days when the judges ruled, that there was a famine in the land. And a certain man of Bethlehem in Judah went to live in the country of Moab—he, his wife, and his two sons. The name of the man was Elimelech, the name of his wife Naomi, and the name of his two sons Mahlon and Chilion. They left their home town, Bethlehem in Judah, and went to live in the country of Moab.

Elimelech, Naomi's husband, died and left her a widow with two sons. The sons married two women of Moab. One was named Orpah, and the other, Ruth. They lived in Moab about ten years longer, then Naomi's sons, Mahlon and Chilion died also, leaving Naomi without her two sons and her husband.

Then she arose with her daughters-in-law, and prepared to leave Moab and return to Judah, for she had heard in the country of Moab how that the Lord had visited his people in giving them bread. So she and her two daughters-in-law left Moab to return to the land of Judah.

Then Naomi said unto her two daughters-in-law, "Go, return each to your mother's house. May the Lord deal kindly with you, as you have dealt with the dead, and with me. The Lord grant you that you may find rest, each of you in the house of your husband." Then she kissed them, and they lifted up their voices and wept. And they said to her, "Surely we will return with you to your people."

Naomi answered them saying, "Turn again, my daughters. Why will you go with me? Are there yet any more sons in my womb, that they may be your husbands? Turn again, my daughters. Go your way, for I am too old to have a husband. If I should say I have hope, if I should have a husband also tonight, and should also bear sons, would you wait for them until they were grown? Would you wait for them instead of marrying? No, my daughters, for it grieves me much for your sakes that the hand of the Lord is gone out against me."

They lifted up their voices and wept again, and Orpah kissed her mother-in-law and left her, but Ruth stayed with her. And Naomi said to Ruth, "Look, your sister-in-law has gone back to her people, and to her gods. Return with her." But Ruth said, "Do not ask me to leave you, or to stop following you. For wherever you go, I will go; and wherever you live, I will live. Your people shall be my people, and your God my God. Where you die, I will die, and there I will be buried. The Lord do so to me, and more also, if anything but death parts you and me."

When Naomi saw that Ruth was determined to go with her, she said no more to her about leaving her.

Divine Impact

Dance with the One Who Brung Ya

Darrell Royal, the very successful football coach at the University of Texas from 1957 to 1976, coined a phrase that tells as well as anything what loyalty means: "Dance with the one who brung ya."

This colloquial expression gets to the heart of the matter. You go with your date to the prom and that's the one you dance with, no matter how strong the temptation to switch to another partner. Coach Royal used the phrase to describe the stance he took about changing players or strategies in a big game. Late in a winning season, with his team in an important game, things didn't always go well. When the Longhorns got behind in the score or his players weren't performing up to their potential, Royal refused to switch players or change strategies that had worked in earlier victories. He made commitments to the players and to his plan, and he didn't waver when things got a little rough. He knew his best bet in the long run was to "dance with the one who brung ya." The results usually proved him right: In 20 seasons

The Family Loyalty of Ruth

Royal chalked up 184 victories and suffered only 60 defeats, winning national championships three times.

In the story of Ruth we find a loyalty that exceeds expectations. It proceeds from a commitment she had made. Ruth married a son of Naomi, obviously taking her vows seriously. She was in it for life.

When her husband died, Ruth chose to remain with her widowed mother-in-law. Later Naomi suggested that Ruth go find a new husband among her own people. There is certainly nothing wrong with that, but Ruth would have none of it. She was determined to remain with her mother-in-law even though it meant moving off to a place where she knew no one else.

When Ruth decided to marry into Naomi's family, it was like taking a loyalty oath. I can imagine her thinking, "This is my family now." And the death of her husband didn't change that. Consistency. Committed today, faithful to that commitment tomorrow.

This is not to suggest that if we are placed into the circumstances of Ruth and Naomi today we should do the same as she did. Loyalty to those to whom we have made commitments can be expressed in different ways in different places and different times. But the principle is the same. Whatever we commit to, we stay with. Being loyal is an expression of that commitment. It goes with the territory. And it applies to the commitments we make in all our relationships: marriage vows, business contracts, treaties among nations, and more.

The story of Ruth can inspire us to be careful when making a commitment, but when we do we are obligated to go all the way in honoring that commitment.

Life Enrichment Axiom 4:

Loyalty means sticking by those to whom we have made commitments, and not switching sides when it seems to be of more advantage to us. In this way we will earn the trust and respect of others.

5

The fear of God makes a hero;
the fear of man makes a coward.
—World War I hero, Sgt.
Alvin York

An Underdog Upsets the Favorite
The Story of David and Goliath

David is one of the great heroes of the Bible. He certainly earned the title of hero when he, a mere boy, killed the mighty Philistine warrior Goliath. This reading from the First Book of Samuel tells the story of how David the shepherd boy single-handedly saved Israel from certain defeat, using only a sling and a stone against the heavily armed and armored giant Philistine, Goliath.

David wasn't drafted into Israel's army; he volunteered. What's more, in his preparation for confronting Goliath, he turned down the offer of armor and a sword, opting instead for his sling—a weapon he had once used to kill a lion and a bear that threatened the sheep he was tending. When he took on Goliath, his display of courage in facing what would appear to be impossible odds was exceeded only by his unquestioning belief in divine support. A man who is blessed with this combination of qualities is a force to be reckoned with.

David and Goliath

First Samuel:
Chapter 17, Verses 20 through 50

David rose up early in the morning, left the sheep with a keeper, and went as Jesse had commanded him. He came to the battlefield just as the army was going forth to the fight, and shouted for the battle. For Israel and the Philistines had put the battle in array, army against army. David left his carriage in the hand of the keeper of the carriage, then ran to the army, found his brothers, and saluted them. As he talked with them, they looked up and saw the champion, the Philistine of Gath, Goliath by name, out of the armies of the Philistines, who repeated the words he had said to them earlier (the challenge to the Israelites to send one man to fight him to settle the battle), and David heard him..

When all the men of Israel saw the man, they fled from him and were very afraid. The men of Israel said, "Have you seen this man? Surely he came to defy Israel. The king will reward whoever kills him with great riches, and will give him his daughter, and make his father's house free in Israel."

David spoke to the men that stood by him,

saying, "What shall be done to the man that kills this Philistine and takes away the reproach from Israel? For who is this uncircumcised Philistine that he should defy the armies of the living God?"

The people answered him, saying, "It shall be just as we said for the man that kills him."

David's oldest brother, Eliab, heard when he spoke to the men; and Eliab's anger was kindled against him.   He said, "Why did you come here? And with whom have you left those few sheep in the wilderness? I know your pride and the naughtiness of your heart; for you came to see the battle." David said, "What have I now done? Is there not a cause?" Then he turned from him to another, and spoke the same words.   And the people answered him again and told him the same thing as before.

When the words were heard which David spoke, they repeated them before Saul and Saul sent for him. David said to Saul, "Let no man's heart fail because of him; your servant will go and fight with this Philistine." And Saul said to David, "You aren't able to go against this Philistine to fight with him, for you are too young and he is a man of war from his youth. David said unto Saul, "Your servant kept his father's sheep, and there came a lion and a bear and took a lamb out of the flock. I went out after the lamb and struck the lion

David and Goliath

and took the lamb out of his mouth. And when the lion attacked me, I caught him by his beard, and struck him again and killed him. Your servant killed both the lion and the bear, and this uncircumcised Philistine shall be as one of them, seeing he has defied the armies of the living God." David also said, "The LORD that delivered me out of the paw of the lion, and out of the paw of the bear, will deliver me out of the hand of this Philistine."

So Saul said to David, "Go, and the LORD be with you."

Saul armed David with his armor and put a helmet of brass on his head; also he armed him with a coat of mail. David put on his sword and because he had never had on armor before, or used a sword, he tried them out. Then he said to Saul, "I cannot go with these for I have never used them." Then he took off all the armor.

Then David took his staff in his hand and chose five smooth stones out of the brook, and put them in a shepherd's bag which he had, even in a scrip. He carried his sling in his hand and approached the Philistine. The Philistine came near David, with a man carrying his shield in front of him. And when the Philistine looked about and saw David, he disdained him, for he was just a boy—ruddy and of a fair countenance.

Divine Impact

The Philistine said to David, "Am I a dog that you came to me with staves?" Then the Philistine cursed David by his gods, and said to David, "Come to me, and I will give your flesh to the fowls of the air and to the beasts of the field."

Then David said to the Philistine, "You come to me with a sword, and with a spear, and with a shield, but I come to you in the name of the LORD of hosts, the God of the armies of Israel whom you have defied. Today the LORD will deliver you into my hand; and I will strike you and take off your head and give the carcases of the host of the Philistines to the fowls of the air and to the wild beasts of the earth, so that all the earth may know that there is a God in Israel. And everyone here shall know that the LORD saves not with sword and spear, for the battle is the LORD'S and he will give you into our hands."

Then when the Philistine arose and went forward to meet David, David hurried and ran toward the army to meet the Philistine. He put his hand in his bag and took out a stone, then slung it, hitting the Philistine in his forehead. The stone sank into his forehead, and he fell face down onto the ground. So David prevailed over the Philistine with a sling and with a stone, and hit the Philistine and killed him, but there was no sword in David's hand.

David and Goliath

The Dynamic Duo—Faith and Courage

In volunteering to face Goliath, David knew that his opponent was formidable. But he seems to have brushed it off as a non-issue, much like a small boy entering a dark alley holding onto his father's hand. The boy has no reason to fear, for his father will protect him from whatever dangers may be lurking in their path. In David's case it was not his earthly father, but his heavenly Father whose hand he was holding. He had every confidence that God would protect him from the enemy and cause him to be victorious. His faith in God's support of Israel and its cause was so great that losing this fight was out of the question—an impossibility. Such faith breeds courage.

Is there a parallel in the twenty first century to the story of David's courage against Goliath? In September 2001, in New York and Washington D.C., there were many who displayed courage. And those who serve in the military, law enforcement or other potentially dangerous public service, regularly put their lives on the line. But most of us never, or rarely, face an enemy that can in any way be compared to Goliath. Opportunities to exhibit moral courage, however, arise often. Such challenges are generally spiritual or psychological in nature.

A half century ago there was a popular comic strip named for the central character, *Pogo*, a talking possum. Pogo maintained that he had "met the enemy and it is us." Indeed, "us" is the enemy we most often face. More specifically, the enemy very often is not something in us, but something *not in us*—some quality which is lacking in our character. Our character flaws may manifest themselves in lethargy, apathy or even cowardice when we are challenged. We may wish for courage to come to our egos' rescue, but if it is not deeply seeded in our character it may well abandon us every time the gauntlet is thrown down in front of us.

To be confident of God's presence and believe that His spiritual resources are available to us through faith gives us a foundation for developing character. Then, by building on that foundation with the regular practice of faithful living, we will prepare ourselves for facing the giant challenges presented by life in the twenty first century.

David and Goliath

Life Enrichment Axiom 5:

When we work at developing a strong faith in God, our character will strengthen and our self-esteem will grow.

6

Rest, rest, perturbed spirit!
—William Shakespeare (in Hamlet)

The Lord is My Escape Hatch
The Twenty Third Psalm

The twenty third Psalm is one of the most beloved and most recited passages in the Bible. It is often used in funeral services to comfort mourners, and is urgently called to mind by those facing imminent danger. Its words are indeed comforting.

The authorship of the twenty third Psalm is attributed to David, whose early life as a shepherd boy is reflected in the metaphors of the Lord as shepherd and of His people as the sheep He cares for. It is a

The Lord is My Escape Hatch

song David may have sung to King Saul in the days before their enmity. He may have used it to prepare the king for an upcoming battle, or perhaps to console him after he had sustained a defeat or received a serious wound. But I can more easily imagine David composing and singing this memorable song for himself, to help him endure the difficulties he faced so many times. In his youthful zeal when facing Goliath, he may not have required such encouragement as the twenty third Psalm offers, but later, as his challengers were not so easily dispatched, he may have seen the need to remind himself of God's constant care.

Today, the twenty third Psalm can offer comfort to us all, not just in times of anguish, but also when we encounter the many harassments that perturb us in our everyday living. These verses offer us a respite from the daily struggles of ordinary life.

Divine Impact

Psalm 23

The LORD is my shepherd; I shall not want. He makes me lie down in green pastures; he leads me beside the still waters. He restores my soul and leads me in the paths of righteousness for his name's sake.

Yea, though I walk through the valley of the shadow of death, I will fear no evil, for you are with me; your rod and your staff comfort me.

You prepare a table before me in the presence of my enemies; you anoint my head with oil; my cup overflows. Surely goodness and mercy shall follow me all the days of my life, and I will dwell in the house of the LORD forever.

The Lord is My Escape Hatch

Stilling the Rampaging Waters
of Modern Life

There could be no more perfect consolation to mourners of the dead, nor more encouraging words for those facing imminent danger or death, than the beautifully written twenty third Psalm. Its words and the imagery they evoke convey the assurance that God is with us at all times and in all places, offering us the peace that passes all understanding. But it can be much more than a cornerstone of funeral oratory or soothing words for the fearful and the suffering. It can be a refreshing spiritual tonic for those of us who too often get caught up in the frenzy of the hectic life of modern society.

When I am worried, anxious, fearful or frustrated by the turmoil of daily life that sometimes engulfs me, I like to retreat from the fray for a few minutes, find a quiet place and read the twenty third Psalm. As I do, I can imagine sitting on the grassy bank of a gently flowing stream without a care in the world. I cannot see the physical presence of God there, as I have no image of God to call up, other than the gray-bearded old man of childhood Sunday school lessons, which I have long since attempted to dispel. Yet I do see God in that peaceful setting. I see Him in the setting itself—calm, peaceful, comforting, unhurried, with all His attention focused on me and my concerns. I am reminded of how much He loves me and wants the best for me. By the best I do not mean worldly success, but the tranquility I experience in these few moments of reverie. Then I am at peace with God and with the world, and have the assurance of eternal life with Him, when nothing will worry or frustrate me.

As I read through the six verses of the Psalm, which I often must do several times before I can keep and hold the imagery evoked by them, I pause and meditate on what each verse means to me. Notice I said "what each verse means to me," as I believe that readers may understand the same words in different ways, depending on their own life experiences. This personalizing of the Psalm allows me to consider how I believe God is helping me deal with my specific concerns.

When He makes me lie down in green pastures, in my mind's eye He comes to my office, takes me by the hand and escorts me outside to a beautiful green meadow, which in my imagination is just outside my back door.

But He doesn't make me lie down just yet. First, He leads me down the green slope of the meadow to the edge of a gently flowing stream. Some may picture a perfectly still pond, but my idea of peace is crystal clear water rippling over smooth stones and emitting a soft, gurgling euphony.

Now He makes me lie down in the green grass, from where I take in all the beauty of the idyllic scene. I breathe in the fresh air and look up to see soft white clouds floating through an azure sky. I turn onto my side, then as I lean on my elbow and chew a blade of grass, I watch the water flow. A few moments of this image and I can feel my energy and enthusiasm begin to return. He is restoring my soul.

When I think of Him leading me in the path of righteousness for His namesake, I am reminded of my priorities—that I must not let worldly cares stand in the way of obediently following the path He has laid out for me. The metaphors of Shepherd and sheep work perfectly as I am shown the way to the fold.

When I read about going through the valley of the

Divine Impact

shadow of death, my mind takes me to a scene from a piece written by J. B. Phillips in which he recounts a dream he had while in a comatose state during a serious illness. He believes it was a near-death experience.

In his dream Phillips is walking down a slope toward a white bridge which spans a small stream. The entire slope is littered with debris of all kinds. The sight of all the mess repulses him. Then when he looks across the bridge to the other side, he sees a perfectly clean and stunningly beautiful Eden. Standing amidst the beauty is a figure in white. As Phillips sees himself running toward the bridge to get to the paradise on the other side, he is pulled up short when the figure in white holds up a hand to halt his progress. The figure lets him know that it is not yet time for him to cross; he must return up the messy slope and remain among the debris for a while longer.

In my meditation on the twenty third Psalm I repeat this scene which J. B. Phillips so graphically describes. It not only assures me that God will carry me through any dark and troubling times I may face, but it also reminds me of what is in store for me at the end. All this gives me an enormous infusion of hope and courage.

To me, the last two verses of the Psalm look ahead to the time when I will cross to the other side of that narrow, gentle stream and enter into Paradise. There, God prepares a feast for me, cleans me up and shows me the abundance of life with Him. With that belief in the ways God treats His people, I am made confident that whatever happens I will enjoy His mercy and goodness all my days, and indeed, will dwell in the House of the Lord forever.

Life Enrichment Axiom 6:

Keeping the Bible near us wherever we are gives us instant access to words of comfort and encouragement.

7

*Never trust a friend who
deserts you in a pinch.*
—Aesop

Who Can You Trust?

Timeless Counsel from Proverbs

Proverbs is one of three books in the Bible which are collectively characterized as "wisdom literature," the others being Job and Ecclesiastes. A reading of these books shows why they are labeled as such. The Book of Proverbs is filled with much good advice that would prove useful to people at any time in human history. But so many of these maxims seem to have a special relevance for the present age. Reading a modern English version of Proverbs today could lead one to believe that much of the advice found there was written recently. It is utterly practical, yet often profound.

The proverb found in Chapter 3, Verses 5 and 6, is a prime example. It has been selected for inclusion here because it has timeless value. It counsels us to place our trust in God rather than rely on our own limited abilities and knowledge. There is no time when that is not good advice, probably the best advice anyone could ever receive.

Divine Impact

Proverbs: Chapter 3, Verses 5 and 6

Trust in the Lord with all your heart and lean not on your own understanding. In all your ways acknowledge him and he shall direct your paths.

Who Can You Trust?

God Is Open for Business

When we are faced with problems and puzzled over what to do, there is a consultant available to help us figure things out. It is God, the Master Consultant, who long ago hung out His shingle and is open for business 24 hours a day, seven days a week.

GOD Unlimited
Consulting for All Human Needs

We mortals struggle with problems of every kind every day. It is necessary. It is life. But there is help available. We can consult with the all-knowing God, who tells us throughout the Scriptures that He wants to help us. All we need to do is call on Him. We don't even need an appointment. If we will take our problems to Him and trust Him to do what is best, He will enable us to deal with the problem.

The key word here is trust. Trusting God to have the right answer is essential because the answer is often, at least in the short term, not what we think it should be—not at all what we want to hear at the time. A similar concept is expressed by the Apostle Paul in the New Testament. In writing his letter to the Christians in Rome in the mid-first century, Paul wrote, "All things work together for good for those who love God." If we *love* God, presumably we also *trust* God. But how can we trust God amidst tragedy, pain or failure? Our natural response to these circumstances is to complain to God—even to curse Him. "How could a loving God let this happen?" we ask.

The short answer to that question is "nobody knows." But on thoughtful reflection we can see that suffering is often due to our collective misuse of free will, giving us a world in which we inflict much pain and suffering on each other—the price we pay for freedom. Still, that answer doesn't explain the suffering caused by natural disasters or by un-preventable diseases for which there is no known cure. No matter what the cause of suffering, God can still bring good out of it. This is what Paul tells us, and this is what the Proverb says. Just trust God and be patient.

Quick relief and total healing are what we want from our suffering, but we don't always get them. There are many cases of suffering, though, that are catalysts for other kinds of good. I have seen cases in which one who suffers brings out the best qualities in family members, friends, and even care givers, evoking in them the compassion and courage they never knew they had. Despite our inability to understand why some who suffer get relief and others do not, we can still trust that God is working His wonders in ways that, over the long haul, will benefit all concerned. And I believe that He will make it up to those who suffer in this life by rewarding them with unimaginable joy in the next.

While I have never had a serious handicap or long term painful illness, I did have an experience that proved to me how God can be trusted to turn a bad situation into a blessing. When I was a young father of four, a fifth child was born into our family. He and his mother had suffered through a difficult birthing process, and he had several congenital orthopedic problems. But with surgical procedures those were manageable.

When he was six months old, however, he was diagnosed as mentally retarded. I was devastated and, as we are prone to do in such circumstances, I blamed

Divine Impact

God. But over the years something totally unexpected happened. I didn't merely come to accept my son's condition, but I also came to realize that he is a profound blessing to me and to just about everyone who knows him. He has an indomitable spirit and a strong faith in God; and he enjoys life like nobody I know. And thanks to the compassion and skills of people in the fields of medicine and social services, he is a healthy, happy and well-adjusted young man. God has taken an extreme disappointment and turned it into a supreme joy.

I wish I could say that I had trusted God from the beginning to make things okay with my son. At that time, of course, I would have expected only that God make my son "normal." Such black and white expectations of God are usually what we have. We don't know what else to ask God for when we pray. But He knows how all things fit together in the big picture, given our human limitations and the laws of nature, which He chooses not to break.

Now, I would not want my son to change in any way. To me and to the other members of our family, he is who he is—a fine young man whom we all love and respect. Along the way, through my son's growth and development, through the ordeals of some seven or eight surgeries, God taught me to trust Him. He knows what He is doing. Why not trust Him with our whole lives?

Life Enrichment Axiom 7:

Trusting God means being patient and waiting to see how, in His wisdom, He works things out.

8

That men do not learn from the lessons of history is the most important of all the lessons history has to teach.
                                            —Aldous Huxley

Will We Ever Learn?
A Dire Warning from a Wise Man of Old

I wish that I had paid more attention to the Book of Proverbs when I was young. There is so much wisdom there—lessons in everything from how to rear and educate children to how to accept old age, and much in between. This pearl of wisdom from Proverbs 29 states a verifiable truth about what happens to a society that will not consider carefully another truth—*what we reap, we sow.* Or, to put it in more specific terms, our casual disregard for God's laws today is

Will We Ever Learn?

likely to come back to haunt us tomorrow. If this proverb was written by King Solomon in the tenth century B.C., as is commonly believed, then humankind has had ample time to learn the lesson it contains. Alas, many of us have not.

Divine Impact

Proverbs 29:18

Where there is no vision, the people are unrestrained.

Will We Ever Learn?

A Vision of Greatness

In Edward Gibbon's classic tome, The History of the Decline and Fall of the Roman Empire, the author describes how moral decay within Rome was one of the causes of the collapse of the empire. After five centuries of world dominance, the proud Romans saw the empire fall apart and Rome itself sink to humble mediocrity. Gibbons lays a fair part of the blame on an increasingly decadent and disorderly citizenry's loss of the vision of what had made Rome great. His premise was essentially that corruption in high places, immorality and civil disobedience so weakened the once-great empire that she became vulnerable to outside forces which had earlier been unable to penetrate the Roman bastions.

Can it happen to us in the twenty first century? Is America doomed to suffer the fate of Rome? Are we possibly showing the first signs of the same sort of moral and civil collapse as did Rome before its fall? It all depends on whether or not we keep our immunization up to date. For the United States to remain the great nation it has always been, we must protect ourselves against the kind of moral decay that led to the ruin of Rome. To do that we must never lose sight of the vision of America's greatness first held by the founding fathers, and sustained, in the more than two centuries since, by a people whose strength of character and moral fiber made the government of the people, by the people and for the people work to fulfill the vision.

This means that we who have inherited the benefits of those who have kept the vision alive must be ever vigilant against the perils of losing our vision of greatness. It is essential that we remember what it takes to sustain our moral strength, which is, I believe, the backbone of our greatness and the foundation of our system of liberty and justice.

The source of that moral strength, of course, is God, the giver of life and the provider of moral laws which He designed for our own good. The writer of the Proverbs knew that and wisely foretold what would happen to nations like Rome. The fall of Rome was a replay of the Sodom and Gomorrah story, albeit with somewhat less novel consequences.

Will We Ever Learn?

We can escape Rome's fate if we remember that God's laws are the underpinnings of human liberty and justice, and must be obeyed. We will reap what we sow. So far we have reaped what the founding fathers sowed, and, while the process hasn't been without some serious challenges, what they sowed has yielded the fruits of freedom, prosperity and domestic tranquility.

If twenty first century Americans and those who follow us keep God's laws, our nation's greatness will continue. It all begins with us, each individual American. If each of us establishes and maintains a vision of personal greatness within the context of our free society, the maintenance of the national vision of greatness will follow as a natural consequence.

Life Enrichment Axiom 8:

With a strong vision of where we want to be in the future, as individuals, as families, and as a nation, and with God as our guide, we will continue to enjoy life, liberty and the pursuit of happiness.

9

*Hope must always be based on realities, and
in the end upon God, the Great Reality.*
                                        —J. B. Phillips

Hang On—Help is on the Way
The Prophet Isaiah Has a Vision of Hope

Whenever we get in trouble and do not know how to get out of it, we look for someone to come to our aid. This is true of individuals, groups and even whole societies. Policemen, firefighters, EMT's, doctors and lawyers answer such calls for help all the time. And when wars or terrorist attacks threaten our safety, our government takes measures to calm our fears.

Knowing that we are not alone in times of crisis, that there are those who will come to our aid, we are

Hang On—Help is on the Way

encouraged to believe that we will survive the crisis and will be able to live out our lives in relative peace. This is hope.

In Old Testament times the people of Israel seemed to be under constant threat of conquest. Of course, they blamed God. The prophets among them would often warn the people that it was their ungodly ways that brought on their troubles, telling them that they must repent if they were to be saved from disaster. But some of the prophets added a message of hope: some time in the future a king would come and rescue them from their troubles.

Isaiah was one of the those prophets who had a gift for such hopeful visions of the future. He wouldn't say when the king would come, so the people had to be patient. But he did present an image of what the king would be like, and promised that when he came he would deliver his people from their woes. The effect of Isaiah's message was essentially, "Hang on—help is on the way."

Divine Impact

Isaiah: Chapter 9, Verses 6 through 8

For unto us a child is born, unto us a son is given; and the government shall be upon his shoulder; and his name shall be called Wonderful, Counselor, The Mighty God, The Everlasting Father, The Prince of Peace. Of the increase of his government and peace there shall be no end, upon the throne of David, and upon his kingdom, to order it, and to establish it with judgement and with justice now and forever.

Hang On—Help is on the Way

Hope, the Forgotten Virtue

When Norman Vincent Peale wrote *The Power of Positive Thinking* in 1952 he touched an American nerve. Our country had always been a nation of positive thinkers. It goes back to those brave souls who colonized this new land. And the Founding Fathers had to "think positive" or they would not have signed the Declaration of Independence. Then came the pioneers, without whose genuine hope for the future the frontier might never have been explored and settled. If they had not crossed the Appalachians and swept westward, the predominant language on the North American continent today might well be Spanish, French, or even Russian. Moreover, without the optimism of the dreamers who built this nation's industrial might, our economy could very well be a century behind what it is today.

It takes positive thinkers, men and women with the so-called "can do" spirit, to make things happen. So when Peale wrote his book, he was merely articulating what had made us into what we already were—a

Divine Impact

strong, prosperous country that spanned the continent. What made the book immensely popular, though, was his message that anyone could still do such things today. John or Jane Doe could succeed at whatever he or she chose, by first believing that success was possible, then maintaining that belief through the course of one's endeavors. What Peale was selling, really, was hope. He was certainly not referring to wishing, quite a different thing, which many confuse with hope. And he made it clear that hope, i.e., positive thinking, was volitional, not just a gift a fortunate few were given at birth. Before anyone ever heard of Nike sport shoes or Michael Jordan, Norman Vincent Peale was telling his readers, *Just do it.*

Peale was a Christian minister who brought the virtue of hope to the public's attention, albeit under the catchy name of positive thinking. But hope has not always been a prominent feature of Christian teaching and sermonizing. In the first century A.D., the apostle Paul wrote a letter to the Corinthians in which he expounded on the virtue of love. In his conclusion to what is often called "The Love Chapter," he mentions faith and hope, along with love, as enduring virtues.

Hang On—Help is on the Way

The last line of that chapter has become one of the most quoted lines from all of Paul's works: *And now these three things endure: faith, hope, and love; but the greatest of these is love.*

Paul's elevation of love over faith and hope rings true, especially if we agree with the Apostle John's statement that "God is love." Of the other two virtues, faith gets plenty of emphasis from religious leaders and writers. But somehow hope seems to get short shrift. In Sunday sermons and religious treatises it often takes a back seat to love and faith. Yet hope is a vital component of joyous living. It deserves more attention. And it should be stressed that hope is, as Norman Vincent Peale said of positive thinking, a virtue to be initiated and regularly practiced, not a genetic personality trait.

To many, hope may mean believing that better times are right around the corner, anticipating the promotion or big raise in pay, or looking forward to a summer vacation. These are just a few examples of the things that are part and parcel of the lives of many ordinary Americans. How much more significant is the coming of a king who brings us peace and justice forever, as

Divine Impact

Isaiah foretold?

While the people of the Jewish faith still await the Messiah's arrival, Christians believe that He has already come. And when He came He brought us much more hope than Isaiah could ever have dreamed about—such as telling us that if we accept Him as our king we will be spending eternity in the joyous presence of God. You can't top that for something to look forward to—to hope for.

Whereas hope is a virtue to be practiced, wishing is mere fantasy. People wish their favorite team would win the championship. They wish for a million dollars. They wish they could go on a cruise around the world. But they do not necessarily really hope for such things. Hope is believing that what you wish for really will come true. Hope keeps us going—believing that the future will be better. Of course, there is a subtle difference between positive thinking and hope. While both are volitional—we choose to think positively, and we choose to hope—thinking positively is an attitude with which we approach life and its problems, whereas hope is a deep-seated belief that what we want to happen will happen. We can think positively about something in the hope that it will come to be.

Our hopes for a better future on earth change as we change. We hope for one thing when we are twenty, quite another when we are sixty. Then when we approach the latter stages of life our hopes shift from earthly desires to eternal ones. This adaptability is God's gift. Young men and women, while believing they will go to heaven when they die, will hardly let that hope dominate their thinking, nor should they. There is life to be lived. Still, if they keep that assurance of eternal bliss in mind, the natural dread of death will be thwarted, and the joyous life may be fully experienced.

Hope is not always easy to conjure up. Suffering from long term serious illness, extreme poverty, or any number of problems life may dish out, can dim our hopes. When there is no hope for a resolution to life's problems, despair is waiting in the wings to choke out our potential for joy. Since life does have its unresolvable problems, we must look beyond this earthly life for a positive outcome. If we are grounded in a strong faith in God and belief in His son, we can indeed have hope for a better future—a future to be lived in a place where problems do not exist.

Divine Impact

Life Enrichment Axiom 9:

When we practice the virtue of hope we open ourselves to life's abundance, both in the present world and in the one beyond.

10

Be prepared.
—Boy Scouts Motto

First Century A.D., Day One
Start Spreading the News

About seven hundred years after Isaiah predicted the coming of a "Wonderful King," it actually happened. The New Testament contains the story of the arrival of the Messiah, what He said and did, and what happened to Him. This passage from Luke tells us about an angel making the announcement of the arrival of the King for whom the whole of Israel had been awaiting for so long. The fact that the angel first told the Good News to a few shepherds rather than to secular or religious leaders was a harbinger of things to come. This King had come to provide hope for the poor, the sick and the downtrodden, not to overthrow governments and rule the world.

Hardly anyone besides the shepherds noticed the arrival of the Messiah. Instead of entering as a mighty conqueror, He came as a baby born in very humble circumstances to parents of no distinction. He grew up in a small country town in Palestine and attracted no attention until He began His ministry at the age of thirty. This Messiah came in humility and taught such odd things as turning the other cheek when struck, offering your shirt to a thief after he had already stolen your coat, and loving your enemies. He wore no golden crown nor did He swing an avenging sword. He did not proclaim Himself to the rulers with any "Step aside, I'm taking over," assertion. Rather, He walked among the poor, teaching them His strange new way of thinking. His only displays of special powers were the miracles He performed in aiding the hungry, the sick, the blind and the lame. Those who had waited in hope for the Messiah expected someone different. Where was the "Wonderful King" who promised to bring peace and justice?

First Century A.D., Day One

As a result of the totally surprising ways of this humble Messiah, many did not accept Him as the Savior they had hoped for. Moreover, the establishment felt threatened by His radical teachings and wanted Him removed. So they killed Him. When two days later He walked out of the tomb where they had buried Him, the only witnesses were His own followers, so the authorities denied that it happened. To them the matter was closed.

But surprise, surprise! It wasn't over at all. This Man, who came back to life after being dead and buried, so inspired His followers that they spread their new faith in Him to the far corners of the then-known world.

It wasn't long before this little band of believers grew in size and influence, as they told everyone the incredibly good news that God had come to the world as a man and that He loved us all enough to die for our sins. For those who believed, one hope had been fulfilled and another was instilled in their hearts. And it all started when a few shepherds started spreading the news.

Divine Impact

Luke: Chapter 2, Verses 8 through 20

There were in the same country shepherds abiding in the field, keeping watch over their flock by night. And the angel of the Lord came upon them, and the glory of the Lord shone round about them; and they were very afraid. The angel said to them, "Fear not, for I bring you good tidings of great joy, which shall be to all people. For unto you is born this day in the city of David a Savior, which is Christ the Lord. And this shall be a sign unto you. You shall find the babe wrapped in swaddling clothes, lying in a manger."

Suddenly there was with the angel a multitude of the heavenly host praising God, and saying, "Glory to God in the highest and on earth peace and good will toward men." And then, after the angels had gone away to heaven, the shepherds said one to another, "Let us now go to Bethlehem and see this thing that has happened which the Lord has made known to us."   Then they hurried to Bethlehem and found Mary and Joseph, and the babe lying in a manger. When they had seen this, they spread the news of what they were told about the child. And all that heard it wondered at those things which were told them by the shepherds.But Mary remembered all these things and pondered them in her heart. Then the shepherds returned, glorifying and praising God for all the things that they had heard and seen, as it was told to them.

Divine Impact

Be Ready for Anything

After waiting for something for six or seven centuries, when it finally arrives you surely don't want to be let down. When you expect a royal personage adorned with jewels and wielding great power, it's a bit of a let-down to discover that the one you had expected is really just an average guy from a working class family, a carpenter by trade.

Then when He leaves home and tours the country teaching weird new ideas, you might naturally assume that he is a charlatan. You know from your history books that this lowly tradesman from the boonies could not be the one that had been promised. How could anyone like this have such gall as to pretend to be the Anointed One, the Son of God, the Savior of the world? Get real.

If this happened today would we believe it? I'm referring to the first appearance of the Son of God, not the reappearance at the end times. Scriptures tell us that the second coming will be different, describing a scenario that should make Him more readily identifiable then, or so we think. But if He had not come before and came among us today as a newborn child, possibly born in a cave, a farmer's barn, a tenement apartment in a big city ghetto, or to use the modern equivalent of the place where Luke tells us Jesus was born—the parking garage of a Holiday Inn—wouldn't we scoff? Or, if we first encountered Him after He reached adulthood and had begun preaching on street corners or in revival tents, wouldn't most of us think of Him as either a pathetic figure or a nutcase?

Without benefit of hindsight to the real first appearance, many of us very likely would pay no attention to Him, with the possible (or probable?) exception of the poor, the disheartened, and the hopeless—in other words, the desperately needful members of our society. Of course, those were the same kinds of people who were attracted to Him when He really did dwell among us.

The inspiration from this passage derives from the fact that God came to us as a man to rescue us from our sins. It is the single most important and wonderful event in history. But it is also inspiring to know that the way God chose to enter the world was as a seemingly ordinary man. Obviously, He was anything but ordinary, but nobody could know that without seeing and hearing Him—or at least hearing about Him from a trustworthy eyewitness. Coming in the way that He did, and reaching out to the neglected and underprivileged, is encouraging to all who recognize their own need of God—both then and now.

There are probably many lessons which can be learned from God's choice of humble circumstances to enter the physical world of humankind, but certainly one of them is that it is very unwise to form rigid opinions about what God might do or how He might do it. If we are aware of our need of Him and watch diligently with an open mind and heart, we will recognize Him. He's the One who brings Good News to anyone who will listen and respond.

Life Enrichment Axiom 10:

Whether we are rich or poor, a leader or a follower, if we recognize that we all need God and earnestly seek Him out, He will be there for us.

11

I would rather live in a world where my life is surrounded by mystery than live in a world so small that my mind could comprehend it.
—Harry Emerson Fosdick

Who Is This Guy?
The Apostle John Explains

When the people of the first century heard the story of Jesus' life and teaching, especially the part about His resurrection from the dead, they had a lot of questions. Who wouldn't? And if rising from the dead wasn't enough to arouse the people's curiosity, the followers of Jesus also claimed that the Man of whom they spoke was the Son of God. This called for some explaining. So in the

Divine Impact

latter part of that first century the apostle John took it upon himself to answer some of their questions. The result was The Gospel According to John. This passage is from the opening chapter.

Most of the people in the Roman Empire then were much influenced by the Hellenistic culture of their time, a culture which was very big on philosophy. The apostle John wanted to be sure he explained who Jesus was in terms people could understand, and since he was writing in Greek, the common written language of the day throughout the Roman Empire, he decided he would use the Greek word *logos* as the most accurate way of describing who Jesus was and is.

Logos is literally translated as "word," but in Greek thought "eternal wisdom" or "God's presence" is closer to what was meant by it. This had real meaning for the philosophically oriented Hellenists of the first century, but in modern English "the Word" has no such significance. So, since John clearly was referring to Jesus Christ, it might be better for us as we read this passage to simply substitute "Jesus Christ" for "the Word."

This passage from the first chapter of John's gospel is really an explanatory prologue to the rest of John's

Who Is This Guy?

story of the life and works of Jesus. It is the apostle's way of explaining who Jesus was before he launched into the full story. It is inspiring not only because it asserts the divine nature of Jesus, but also because of the magnificence of its lyrical style. It is truly a beautiful piece of writing. See if you are not strongly affected by this passage.

Divine Impact

John: Chapter 1, Verses 1 through 14

In the beginning was the Word, and the Word was with God, and the Word was God. The same was in the beginning with God. All things were made by him, and without him nothing that exists was made. In him was life, and the life was the light of men. And the light shines in darkness and the darkness did not comprehend.

There was a man sent from God, whose name was John. The same came for a witness, to bear witness of the Light, that all men through him might believe. He was not that Light, but was sent to bear witness of that Light. That was the true Light which lights every man that comes into the world. He was in the world and the world was made by him, and the world did not know him. He came unto his own, and his own received him not. But as many as received him, to them he gave power to become the sons of God, even to them that believe on his name—which were born, not of blood, nor of the will of the flesh, nor of the will of man, but of God.

And the Word was made flesh and dwelt among us, and we saw his glory, the glory of the only begotten of the Father, full of grace and truth.

Who Is This Guy?

Explaining the Unexplainable

God is a mystery. No matter how much we claim we know about Him, or how spiritually close to Him we might feel, we can only begin to accept His multi-dimensional character through Scriptures and faith-based speculation. John is the only one of the four gospel writers who made a point of explaining the concept of the oneness of the Father and the Son. His understanding that Jesus was actually God was the seed of the formation of the Doctrine of the Trinity, a cornerstone of the Church. But no matter how brilliant John's insight, or how wise the wisdom of the later Church council which decided on the Doctrine of the Trinity, we are still left with a mystery. Who can truly understand three persons in one? Let's face it, it's still a mystery. Although John's explanation is credible for those who believe that the accounts of Jesus' life, death and resurrection are true, it is not really understandable as say, two plus two are four, or that the pull of gravity makes objects fall. So we accept it as the mystery that it is. Would it help to rewrite John's explanation in terms more familiar to modern readers who are centuries

Divine Impact

removed from the strong Hellenist influences of John's day? As I brought up in the introduction to this chapter, calling Jesus Christ "The Word" doesn't mean quite the same to us now, at least not without studying the background. To clearly instruct us twenty first century Americans as to who Jesus was and is, a writer would more than likely use terms more common to our culture than "the Word." This may be one of those Bible passages that is better understood by reading one of the paraphrased versions. In The Living Bible, for example, the first three verses read like this:

> *Before anything else existed, there was Christ, with God. He has always been alive and is himself God. He created everything there is—nothing exists that he didn't make.*

This choice of terminology and phrasing makes the writing easier to understand, but does little to give us the kind of understanding that we have of observable facts. But what do we expect from an omniscient, omnipotent, omnipresent God? Should He do things only in ways we can easily understand? Hey, who's in charge here?

God's magnitude is expressed in many ways. One is in the mysteries of the workings of the universe, which humankind may someday come to understand. Another way is in the enigmatic complexity of the species human, a puzzle we will probably never solve. Consider our capacity for creating, our appreciation of beauty and our natural bent toward seeking the truth. Science may explain how we get brown eyes or blue eyes, but it tries in vain to explain those more ethereal traits that separate humans from other animals. So let us not disparage mysteries. They can keep us off the streets and out of trouble while we try to figure them out.

This passage reminds me that God is so far superior to us that we cannot ever truly understand Him. We must simply trust Him.

We've already agreed that God is an awesome God, having read the Genesis story of creation and been sufficiently impressed by the immensity of our star-studded universe and the majestic beauty of our planet. Here's why we need to be reminded of God's awesomeness in this new context: In the Genesis story God the father, the creator, is the one who does all the work. There is no mention of the other two persons of the Trinity. So John has attributed to God the additional dimension of Christ to add to our understanding of the Creator.

Then, in places in the gospel, and in the letters of Paul, we learn that the Holy Spirit is also part of God. Christians now understand God as having three aspects, not just one. He is not only Creator (Father of all creation and of every person), but He has also entered the history of the world as a man, and continues to live among us as spirit. Mystery though it may be, this is what Christians earnestly believe and have a reasonable amount of evidence to prove, although not the kind of evidence that would satisfy scientific protocol.   We now believe in an even larger, more awesome God than we previously knew about. So let us once again ponder the awesomeness of God.

Life Enrichment Axiom 11:

Let the mysteries of God help remind us that He is beyond our understanding and that we are to simply trust Him to do what is best in the long run.

12

Every happening, great and small, is a parable whereby God speaks to us, and the art of life is to get the message.
—Malcolm Muggeridge

The Ultimate Experience

Luke's Story of the Revelation of Simeon

Simeon is one of the least known inspirational figures in the New Testament. At the time of the birth of Jesus, Simeon was already well up in years. He was one of those who had waited expectantly for the coming of the Messiah. But he was exceptional in that he recognized the Messiah when he saw Him, even though Jesus was just seven days old at the time.

Imagine that! What gave this man such insight?

Divine Impact

Faith? Yes, but a special kind of faith. He was so in tune with God, so connected to God's will and His plan for us that God sent His own Spirit to let Simeon know that he would see the Messiah with his own eyes before he died. Then when the blessed event actually came, the Holy Spirit told Simeon that the Messiah had indeed arrived on earth! Not only that, but the Spirit also informed the devout Simeon exactly where he could find the one week-old Savior.

When Simeon, with his familiarity with God and His ways, found Jesus, he did not need to see an I.D. card or fingerprints to be sure this little baby was the One. He recognized Him immediately.

Simeon's response to seeing God in the form of an infant human is inspiring. His life had been fulfilled. He had just had the ultimate experience.

The Ultimate Experience

Luke: Chapter 2, Verses 25 through 33

There was a man in Jerusalem whose name was Simeon and who was a just and devout man. He was waiting for the consolation of Israel and the Holy Spirit was with him. And it was revealed to him by the Holy Spirit that he should not see death before he had seen the Lord's Christ. The Spirit led him into the temple, and when the parents brought in the child Jesus, to do for him after the custom of the law, Simeon took him up in his arms and blessed God, and said, "Lord, now let your servant depart in peace, according to your word. For my eyes have seen your salvation, which you have prepared before the face of all people—a light to lighten the Gentiles, and the glory of your people Israel." And Joseph and his mother marveled at those things which were spoken of him.

Turn Your Radio On

Some readers may recall a song about staying tuned to God that Ray Stephens recorded a few years back. The song is called, "Turn Your Radio On." The lyrics include these lines:

Don't you know that everybody's a radio receiver,
All you gotta do is listen for the call.
Turn your radio on, Turn your radio on.
                    and...
Turn your lights down low and listen to the
     Master's radio,
Get in touch with God, Turn your radio on.

Tuning in to God—staying in close touch with Him—is prerequisite to living well, in the truest sense of the word "well." And I can think of no more apt analogy than turning your radio on—AND tuning to the right station. God's words are always available to us. He broadcasts His messages of hope and love to all of us 24 hours a day, 365 days a year. What's more, He also narrowcasts His very personal signals to us on

The Ultimate Experience

our own private frequency.

But how can we hear any of God's messages if we are tuned in to the wrong station? Wrong stations are often identified by sounds that subtly lure listeners into believing they are hearing good messages, but who then learn at sign-off time that they had been cruelly deceived by the programmer's skill. At the end of the day, the music on the wrong stations always turns discordant. A clue to knowing the station is the wrong one is the annoying static that occasionally interrupts the station's signal. But the longer you stay tuned to it the more acclimated to the noise you become, and eventually the static mixed with the now discordant sounds of the station seems normal.

In contrast, God's station, while not always easy to find, is a clear channel with a signal as strong and crystal clear as we can stand. The best way to get His signal is to just hit the "seek" button.

Other lines in Ray Stephens' song speak to the programming on God's station:

> *Well, come and listen in to a radio station*
> *where the mighty hosts of heaven sing,*
> *Turn your radio on, Turn your radio on.*
> *If you want to feel those good vibrations,*

coming from the joy that His love can bring,
Turn your radio on, Turn your radio on.

Sounds like a station we should all stay tuned to. Simeon inspires me to do that.

Life Enrichment Axiom 12:

If we think of prayer as the tuner in our built-in radio, we can find God's frequency, tune out the static of worldly distractions, and hear God's message of joy, peace, hope and love.

13

It ain't over 'til it's over.
—Yogi Berra

There's a New Day Coming
The Beatitudes

The Beatitudes is a Sunday School-sounding label for Jesus' opening remarks in His "Sermon on the Mount." Whole books have been written about the Beatitudes, reflecting a variety of interpretations of their meaning. These verses can indeed be puzzling, and some Bible readers consider them too depressing or unrealistic to think about. But to me they constitute a powerful message of consolation to all who suffer in this life—a promise that there is a new day coming in which suffering will turn to joy. As you read these verses, see if you get the same feeling of comfort and hope that I do when I read them.

There's a New Day Coming

Matthew: Chapter 5, Verses 1 through 12

Seeing the multitudes, he went up on a mountain, and when he was set, his disciples came to him. Then he began to teach them, saying:

Blessed are the poor in spirit, for theirs is the kingdom of heaven.

Blessed are they that mourn, for they shall be comforted.

Blessed are the meek, for they shall inherit the earth.

Blessed are they which hunger and thirst after righteousness, for they shall be filled.

Blessed are the merciful, for they shall obtain mercy.

Blessed are the pure in heart, for they shall see God.

Blessed are the peacemakers, for they shall be called the children of God.

Blessed are they which are persecuted for righteousness sake, for theirs is the kingdom of heaven.

Blessed are you when others revile you and persecute you and say all manner of evil against you falsely for my sake. Rejoice and be very glad, for great is your reward in heaven; for the prophets before you were also persecuted.

Divine Impact

The Jury is Still Out

If the word "blessed" is better translated in today's English as "happy," as has been expressed in some modern versions of the Bible, then the Beatitudes seem to say that those who suffer in this life are entitled to be happy in the next.

The first Beatitude is exemplary of the others: Blessed are the poor in spirit, for theirs is the Kingdom of Heaven. When Jesus says "theirs is the Kingdom of Heaven," I believe He is referring to the assurance they may rightfully have in the knowledge that they will receive an eternal happiness—the poor in spirit in the here and now will receive their joy in heaven later.

What does it mean, though, to be "poor in spirit?" It could mean humble (a virtue) or depressed (a feeling of hopelessness). It could even mean the sort of submissiveness required of those in poverty. Whatever Jesus intended, I believe that any of the three possibilities fit the gist of the message.

But I do not believe that this or any of the other Beatitudes should be interpreted as a method to use in the pursuit of happiness in this world. Rather, these statements by Jesus assure us that God will make it up later to those who find themselves in difficult circumstances now. That is God's work, not ours.

Obviously for us to accept these things we must believe that there will be a life beyond this one. Only by faith can we take consolation from the Beatitudes. And with that faith we can take anything this life dishes out.

Life Enrichment Axiom 13:

When we become weighed down by the troubles of this world, let us take heart by remembering that God will balance the scales later.

14

The greatest discovery of my generation is that human beings can alter their lives by altering their attitudes of mind.
                              —William James

You Are What You Think

Revolutionary Ideas of Sin

As He continues His Sermon on the Mount, Jesus shocks us with more startling ideas. In the same fifth chapter of Matthew where we read the Beatitudes, He teaches His followers that sin involves more than just what we *do* to hurt others. We can sin by just *thinking* about doing those wrongs. It's His way of telling us that our attitudes toward others is critical—that we must not merely refrain from committing wrong acts, but we must so alter our attitudes that committing those acts is no longer an option for us. This is much to ask of us mere mortals. After all, humans have this basic character flaw called sinful nature, a predilection for doing our own thing while ignoring God's commandments. Remember the Genesis story of The Fall?

What inspires me when I read these verses is the clarity with which Jesus makes plain the path He wants us to travel. Is it easy? Certainly not. Is it hard work? Sure is. But can we complain of not knowing what He expects of us? I don't think so. See what you think as you read.

Divine Impact

Matthew: Chapter 5,
Verses 21 and 22; 27 and 28

(Vss 21-22)

You have heard it said in times past, 'You shall not kill; and whoever kills shall be in danger of the judgment.' But I say to you that whoever is angry with his brother without cause shall be in danger of the judgement...

(Vss 27-28)

You have heard it said in times past, 'You shall not commit adultery.' But I say to you that whoever looks on a woman to lust after her has committed adultery with her already in his heart.

You Are What You Think

The Scarlet Question Mark

In Nathaniel Hawthorne's classic novel, The Scarlet Letter, Hester Prynne was caught in an adulterous affair with the local preacher. The town of Salem where they lived sentenced her to wear a large red letter "A" on the front of her dress. This was the outward and visible sign of an inward and invisible disgrace, to invert a phrase, that revealed her sin to all in the community.

Today such punishment would be ludicrous, but if enforced might lead to a booming business for manufacturers of big red A's. But what if every time married people even thought about having sex outside of marriage they would be made to wear the scarlet "A" in a prominent place on their persons? Scarlet letter makers' stock would skyrocket.

When Jimmy Carter was running for president he was interviewed by *Playboy* magazine. The very fact that he consented to an interview by the magazine, known for displaying pictures of nude women, was a shock to many of Carter's admirers. During the interview, the subject of sex came up and Carter admitted that he had "lusted in my heart." Carter, a married man, knew his Scripture and knew that he had committed a sin when he "lusted in his heart," even though he had not confessed to actually having had sex outside of his marriage.

I wonder if Carter had actually contemplated adultery, or if he was simply admitting to the fact that he had looked at an attractive woman and found her desirable. It seems to me that what Jesus meant by committing adultery in your heart meant actually considering an adulterous act, not just appreciating the attractiveness of a particular member of the opposite sex. I do not believe that Jesus would deny our sexuality or our natural attractions. After all, God designed the whole scheme. To me, the point Jesus was trying to make was that it must end there—that our spiritual self must always rule our physical self, the basis for all self-discipline. If we do not control our urges at that early stage, our appreciation may turn to lust, which may then turn to serious contemplation of a sexual act with the object of our attention. That is when it has gone too far, for if we allow that, Jesus seems to say, then we actually *intend* to pursue having a sexual affair. The only reason we would not, then, would be the fear of getting caught, a poor reason for avoiding any illicit behavior. The sooner we get off the adultery express, the easier our conscience, and the happier our marriage, will be.

In other parts of the gospels Jesus instructs us to love others in the same way we naturally love ourselves. It seems to me that these verses from the Sermon on the Mount give us the fundamentals of how to do that. Before we can truly treat others as we treat ourselves, we must adopt the same attitudes toward them as we have toward ourselves.

The crux of the matter is the problem of unselflessness of our attitude toward other people—female and male alike. Do we harbor bad thoughts about ourselves and wish we could do our own bodies harm if only we wouldn't get caught? Of course not! We give ourselves the benefit of the doubt and plenty of latitude. (I am not speaking here of healthy self-criticism as a means to self-improvement, nor am I referring to psychotic self-loathing.)

While Jesus' two examples in these verses are limited to murder and adultery, He is clearly saying that

Divine Impact

God's laws may not be violated in either *thought* or *deed*. If we take Jesus at His word that either thinking seriously about doing something wrong or actually doing it are both wrong, then it seems to me that many of us had better get back to the drawing board; there's work to be done on our attitudes. And there doesn't seem to be much room for smugness just because we don't act on our lewd or hateful thoughts. We must take self-control to the next level. All the way to the heart.

Life Enrichment Axiom 14:

While we cannot always control the thoughts that enter our heads, by asking God to remove them when they do not glorify Him, He will, in time, show us how to control the tendencies.

15

There is nothing wrong with possessing riches,
but the wrong comes when riches possess men.
—Billy Graham

The Great Investment Banker
in the Sky
Jesus Advises on Wise Investing

Wouldn't it be nice if Jesus had left us advice on how to make safe, profitable investments? Well, He did. His wise investment counsel is found in the Sermon on the Mount. Jesus' recommendations include no tips on any specific stock or bond or CD or IRA. He doesn't even mention Wall Street. To invest God's way is a whole lot different from "beating the street."

Divine Impact

A unique feature of God's idea of a good investment is that you don't even need money. But the really best part is that you reap terrific dividends. Such a deal!

Read on. But beware, you might have to exchange your currency before you can do business with the Great Investment Banker in the Sky.

The Great Investment Banker in the Sky

Matthew: Chapter 6, Verses 19 through 34

Lay not up for yourselves treasures on earth, where moth and rust corrupt and where thieves break in and steal, but lay up for yourselves treasures in heaven, where neither moth nor rust corrupts and where thieves do not break in nor steal.   For where your treasure is, there your heart will be also.

No man can serve two masters, for either he will hate the one and love the other, or else he will hold to the one and despise the other. You cannot serve God and money.

Therefore, I say to you, take no thought for your life, what you will have to eat or what you will have to drink, nor should you be concerned about what you will have to wear.

Isn't there more to life than food and clothing?

Look at the birds of the air. They do not plant, nor harvest, nor gather into barns. Yet your heavenly Father feeds them. Aren't you much better than they? Which of you by taking thought can add one inch to your height? And why worry about clothes? Consider the lilies of the field, how they grow. They do not struggle or worry. Yet I say to you that even Solomon in all his glory was not arrayed like one of these.   So, if God so clothes the grass of the field, which today grows but tomorrow is cast into the oven, won't He clothe you even better, oh you of little faith?

Therefore, do not worry, saying 'What will we have to eat?' or, 'What will we have to drink? or, 'How will we get clothes? (These are the things the Gentiles seek.); for your heavenly Father knows that you need all these things. But seek first the kingdom of God and his righteousness, and all these things shall be provided for you.

The Great Investment Banker in the Sky

Rich Man, Poor Man

The old saying, You can't take it with you, is certainly true of material wealth. But what we can take with us, or more accurately, what we most certainly will take with us, are the leanings of our hearts. Have we laid up treasures on earth or in heaven? Have we loved money and possessions or have we loved God? Jesus makes it abundantly clear in this passage that we cannot have it both ways. We must make a choice.

Is money really the root of all evil? No. The actual quote from Paul's first letter to Timothy is "The love of money is the root of all evil." There is a considerable difference. Money used charitably or wisely can provide many benefits for the general welfare, whereas the love of money can lead to discord, personality disintegration, crime, and paradoxically, poverty—and that's just in this life. The love of money produces such disastrous results because, like the love of anything, it tends to consume our entire being, thus replacing the One to whom we should award those exclusive rights.

That is why Jesus tells us so plainly that we must choose who will be the master we serve, God or money. To me, this does not mean that we must eschew money. We just have to keep it in its right place—as a medium of exchange. What we exchange it for, of course, is what reveals where our hearts are.

We may pile up material goods for any of several reasons: to make us feel more important than others, to indulge our desires for luxury, or to give us what we consider security.

Another option is open to us. We may generously share with those who, through no fault of their own, have little or nothing. The choice is ours. Jesus goes on to say that God will provide for our needs, so we needn't worry about not having enough.

This passage, like others among my selected 25, is really about trusting our fates to God rather than relying on our own resources. When Jesus tells us that we should not worry how we will provide for ourselves, He is saying trust God for all our needs.

God does indeed take care of our needs, although He requires our cooperation. He provides the seed, the sun and the rain to grow food, but we still have to plant, tend, and harvest the crop, then prepare it for eating. He also requires us to share our abundance with those who have needs. That is the way He provides for the poor, the hungry, the homeless—through the rest of us. Clearly, God decided early on that life sustenance was to be a corporate effort. If enough of us are good stewards of God's abundance there will be ample sustenance for all. But if we choose to love money rather than loving God, sharing is very difficult. It's sort of like a camel going through the eye of a needle, to which Jesus once compared a rich man's chances of entering the Kingdom of heaven. Jesus was not saying that a rich man could not get into heaven. He simply used the hyperbole of a camel going through the eye of a needle to illustrate the point that for a rich man it would be more difficult. But He explained later that "with God, all things are possible."

Jesus made these comments just after He had told a rich man how he could become a follower. He told him to sell all that he had and give the money to the poor. The man's response is revealing. He could not do what Jesus asked him to do. Instead, "he went away grieving for he had many possessions."

Not all rich people are in love with money. One of the most generous, loving Christians I know is a man of significant wealth. He no more loves money than he loves a nest of rattlesnakes. But he sees it as an instrument for serving God. He helps those with critical needs as well as those who simply need a little boost. If Jesus confronted him and asked him to sell all that he had and give the money to the poor he would do it in a New York minute. In fact he is doing better than that. He is using his business acumen to provide continuing help to many. As God continues to replenish his abundance, this faithful servant continues to share it with others. He has his priorities straight. He loves God and people; money is merely a medium of exchange. What he exchanges his money for reveals where his treasure lies. He trades it for the encouragement of those in need.

John A. Sanford, in The Kingdom Within, clarifies the problem of wealth:

> *The danger of wealth is not that it automatically excludes the one who possesses it from the kingdom, but that it greatly strengthens the outer mask and inflates the ego. By giving a person a feeling of power, influence, and regard among others, it makes it difficult for him or her to achieve*

The Great Investment Banker in the Sky

> *the inner humility and admission of spiri-*
> *tual need that are prerequisites to a gen-*
> *uine personality...it is not having wealth*
> *as such that destroys our relationship but*
> *what it can do to us if we are unconscious*
> *of its dangers.*

Just as all wealthy people are not in love with money, neither is the love of money the exclusive domain of the rich. Many of us who have little or no wealth may spend much of our lives chasing the almighty dollar. Some catch it, most do not. The price of the pursuit may be steep: poor health, premature death, forfeiture of family life, or even the loss of one's soul.

It is imperative that we place our earthly endeavors in their proper context and not get too concerned about bank balances, interest rates or stock prices, except in terms of being good stewards. If we become obsessed by making and hoarding money, we are apt to jump out of a tall building when things go sour. As Jesus repeatedly says in this passage, there's more to life than material goods. Much more.

Still, there is much I do not understand about how

this passage applies to us in twenty first century America.   Where do we draw the line between providing for our families and sharing with others? What is unnecessary luxury? Especially in a rich country like the United States, these are questions we must ask and seek God's answers. At every turn in examining Scripture we seem to run into the same message, going all the way back to the story of the Fall: God wants us to stay in constant touch with Him. One way He apparently believes that will be accomplished is by our total reliance upon Him for all our needs—one day at a time, seeking His wisdom in dealing with every issue, every question we face. How to handle our financial affairs is no exception.

Investing, like spending, can reveal where our treasures lie. Despite my tongue-in-cheek comments about investments in the introduction to this passage, I am not suggesting that anyone shy away from conventional investing. The point of the passage, though, is obvious: We cannot let our financial affairs become our god. We must always stay on the alert against such an altogether too easy transfer of allegiances. "You cannot serve two masters," is a truism that Jesus recognized, and with which we disagree at our own peril.   If we seek God's help in everything, we can avoid the pitfall of falling in love with money.

Life Enrichment Axiom 15:

By worshiping God and not material possessions, we will gain the necessary wisdom to handle our finances in ways which provide for ourselves, our families and the needs of others.

16

If God wants us to do a thing, he should
make his wishes sufficiently clear.
—Samuel Butler

The Rules Are Simple
(But Not Easy)

Jesus Reduces the Ten Commandments
to Just Two

Jesus had an amazing ability to get straight to the heart of a matter. He simplified things so well. And there was plenty that needed simplification. The Jewish religion of Jesus' time was complicated with an overabundance of detailed legal requirements. Over the centuries after Moses brought the Ten Commandments down from Mount Sinai, religious leaders added hundreds of additional requirements to

The Rules Are Simple

the Jewish canon. By the time Jesus entered the scene, Jews were burdened by an elaborate, complicated system of religious laws, to say nothing of laws imposed by the occupying Romans. In this short passage from the gospel of Matthew, Jesus reduces all religious law—not just the Ten Commandments, but all of it—to two simple requirements. These two commandments, recorded by Matthew, make it clear what God really expects from us.

Divine Impact

Matthew: Chapter 22, Verses 34 through 40

When the Pharisees heard that Jesus had put the Sadducees to silence, they gathered together. Then one of them, a lawyer, asked Him a question, tempting Him, and saying, "Master, which is the great commandment in the law?"

Jesus said to him, "You shall love the Lord your God with all your heart, and with all your soul, and with all your mind. This is the first and great commandment. And the second is like it: You shall love your neighbor as yourself. On these two commandments hang all the law and the prophets."

The Rules Are Simple

Simplify, Simplify

Davy Crockett, the legendary Tennessee frontiersman, and later, defender of the Alamo, is well-known for many things. One of those is a homespun aphorism he was said to have used as a litmus test for any action he considered taking. He advised others to use it, too: "First be sure you're right, then go ahead." Whether or not he was conscious of it, Crockett's method of determining what action to take was based on an idea Jesus inferred in His two great commandments.

In the first century when Jesus simplified the law for His followers, He was probably aware of how complicated details can stultify the human soul. He told them that the hundreds of laws they had been told to obey could really be reduced to two. Had He carried the idea further, He might have asked, "How can you steal, murder, covet, etc., if you love your neighbors as you love yourself? How can you not honor your father and mother if you love them? How can you worship other gods if you love the real One with all your heart, soul, and mind?"

Divine Impact

Seems simple doesn't it? Well, yes and no. The problem lies not in the grosser crimes we might commit, but in the many everyday decisions we must make that involve choices less clear-cut than whether or not to steal or kill or cheat on one's spouse.

When Jesus reduced the law to two simple rules, He took Davy Crockett's aphorism a step further. Crockett said, "Be sure you're right, then go ahead." But he didn't tell us how we can be sure we are right. Jesus gave us a way to determine if we are right without our having to remember a thousand laws.

To test the rightness of what we intend to do we might simply ask ourselves, "Is this the loving thing to do?" Or, stated another way, "Does it demonstrate love for my neighbor and for God?" If we can answer the question positively, then we are clear to "go ahead;" if not, then we try to think of another way to respond to the situation at hand.

Asking the question is a simple way to examine our conscience and be consistent in the application of our values. However, it is not always easy to discern the right answer. There are times when the situation is too complex for us mere mortals to decide what is the loving thing. Often it seems that whatever we choose to do will be the lesser of two evils. Seldom is it the better of two goods, but that, too, makes our decision tough to make.   After years of struggling with these sorts of dilemmas, we start wishing for simpler times—times when life was not so complicated.   So we look back nostalgically to the halcyon days of youth, or even further back into historical times.

One of my sons wishes he had been born two centuries ago, a time when he could live a simpler life, without the hassles of traffic jams, crowded stores, telemarketers, ubiquitous advertising pitches, and other such irritations encountered more or less everyday in urban America today. I am certain that if our ancestors could speak to my son, they would enlighten him somewhat on the "goodness" of the "good old days." Still, his longings have merit. And they are shared by many.

My brother shares a similar dream, although he does have some chance of realizing his. He is just a few years from retirement from a desk job and is planning to escape to a little cabin in the woods as far from civilization as he can get. As might be expected, the role model for his planned future is Henry David Thoreau.

Divine Impact

Thoreau lived in what we realize now was a simpler time, although to him mid-nineteenth century was not simple enough. Walden, published in 1854, became Thoreau's classic how-to book for those who seek isolation from overcivilized society. In it he wrote:

> *Simplicity, simplicity, simplicity! I say let your affairs be as two or three, and not a hundred or a thousand; instead of a million count half a dozen, and keep your accounts on your thumbnail.*

Living apart from society, as Thoreau did for a time, may be a way to simplify our lives, but we can't all do that, nor should we. We may well need to retreat from society for a period of time to reenergize ourselves, or we may even be called to the ascetic life as a way of living for God. But for most of us who accept Jesus' commandments as our guide to living, we are obliged to remain in community and make ourselves available to do what we can to help others who may need us. But even though we may wish to do more to serve our communities, we often find that we are too busy or too tired from our busy-ness to do much. If we will simplify our lives, we will have more time and energy to serve the needs of others. Our help may be material, it may be in service, or it may be in simply visiting the sick or the friendless. I am reminded of an old Sunday School song, "Brighten the Corner Where You Are." I think the song was telling us to do whatever we can wherever we are to make others' lives better. If we will uncomplicate our daily lives, we can make ourselves available for service.

Life Enrichment Axiom 16:

Simplifying our lives to the extent we can allows us to focus more on our relationships with God, family and neighbor.

17

We are weak but He is strong.
—A line from the
Children's song,
Jesus Loves Me

Rest for the Weary

Jesus Offers a Trade

These three verses in Matthew's gospel are some of the most inspiring in all of Scripture. Jesus makes an offer that none of us in our right mind would refuse: to trade in our heavy load for His light one. If He means what I think He means—that we can unload the troubles we are dealt by this world and which weigh us down, in exchange for His light burden of obeying His two simple rules—then who wouldn't want to do that?

Rest for the Weary

Unfortunately, there are many who don't even know about the offer, and others who know about it but don't believe His burden is as light as He would have us think.

In the previous chapter, we read in Matthew 22 that Jesus asks us to follow just two simple rules in order to be His followers: love God with all our hearts, souls and minds and love our neighbors as we love ourselves.

In this passage Jesus tells us that by adopting those rules and making them our way of life (taking on His light burden), we will find rest from our troubles and life will be more joyous for us. After you read this passage, see if you're not ready to dump on His strong shoulders all the back-breaking, brain-scrambling, soul-polluting flotsam and jetsam we carry around with us, and let Him show us how to really live.

Divine Impact

Matthew: Chapter 11, Verses 28 through 30

Come to me all you that labor and are heavy laden, and I will give you rest. Take my yoke upon you and learn from me; for I am meek and lowly in heart, and you shall find rest for your souls. For my yoke is easy and my burden is light.

Rest for the Weary

Lighten Your Load

One possible way to interpret this saying by Jesus is that He, speaking as He was to a people burdened with numerous legal restrictions, was promising His followers relief from such harassment. He might have essentially been saying, "My way isn't like that at all. My way is easy, try it, you'll like it." But for me in twenty first century America it is more instructive to think of Jesus giving me relief from difficult, on-going, unrewarding toil—like giving me a parole from a prison chain gang.

Anyone who has had to endure hard physical labor knows how it feels to be bone tired. All you can think about in such times is getting a hot shower and climbing into bed. Even if we have not worked hard physically, most of us have probably carried a heavy emotional burden at one time or another. It is likely, therefore, that we can all understand what it is like to be heavy-laden. When we work hard and still can't make things come out right, despair may soon follow. Regardless of what Jesus intended when He spoke these words, today the words speak to the despair of those whose labor seems to yield them nothing, whose efforts to lead honest, decent lives are frustrated by hardship or difficulties of various kinds. He tells us that He is ready to give us rest from the trials and tribulations of this life. Sounds good to me.

Life Enrichment Axiom 17:

When we turn our troubles over to God we are freed from despair and discontent.

18

We pardon to the extent we love.
—Francois, Duc de la Rochefoucald

A Father's Patience
And a Rebellious Son's Hard Lesson

The parable of the prodigal son has been called the greatest short story ever told. I agree. And while the gospel writer Luke is the one who wrote down the story, it was originally told by Jesus to illustrate the quality of God's love for us.

Of all the inspiring passages in the Bible, this one stands at or near the top. It is inspiring because the love and forgiveness the father in the story has for his reckless son gives us assurance that our wayward ways will not separate us from the love of God. When

we are finished with wandering and wasting ourselves in worldly pursuits and are ready to return,
God will be there with open arms waiting for us.

A Father's Patience

Luke: Chapter 15, Verses 11 through 32

Jesus said, "A certain man had two sons. The younger of them said to his father, `Father, give me the portion of goods that I will inherit.' So he divided his property between his two sons. Not many days after that the younger son took all his inheritance and traveled to a far country. There he wasted his substance with riotous living. When he had spent all of it, there arose a mighty famine in that land; and he began to be in want. And he went to work for a citizen of that country, who sent him to his fields to feed the hogs. He would have gladly filled his belly with the husks that the hogs ate, but when he realized what a mistake he had made, he said, 'How many hired servants of my father's have bread enough and to spare, and I am dying of hunger! I will arise and go to my father and will say to him, Father, I have sinned against heaven and before you, and I am no longer worthy to be called your son. Make me like one of your hired servants.' And he arose, and went to his father. But when he was yet a great way off, his father saw him and had compassion. He ran to greet his son and embraced and kissed him.

The son said to him, 'Father, I have sinned against heaven and in your sight, and I am no longer worthy to be called your son.' But the father said to his servants, 'Bring out the best robe and put it on him; and put a ring on his hand and shoes on his feet.

And bring the fatted calf and kill it; and let us eat and be merry. For my son was dead, and is alive again; he was lost, and is found.' And they began to be merry.

Now his elder son was in the field, and as he came near the house he heard music and dancing. He called one of the servants and asked what these things meant. And the servant said, 'Your brother has come and your father has killed the fatted calf because he has received him safe and sound.' The older brother became angry and would not go in. So his father came out and asked him to come in. But he said to his father, 'All these years I have been serving you, and I have never failed to obey you, and yet you never gave me even a young goat so that I could make merry with my friends. But as soon as my brother comes home, who has used up all that you gave him on whores, you killed the fatted calf.'

The father answered him, 'Son, you are always with me and all that I have is yours. It was right for us to make merry and be glad, for your brother was dead and is alive again. He was lost and has been found.'"

A Father's Patience

To Err is Human, to Forgive, Divine

This familiar line by Alexander Pope hits the nail on the head. We mortals can make up all kinds of ways to sin against humankind and against God. Then after the fact we are adept at making up excuses. We dismiss our errant behavior as necessary for survival, or as a result of experiencing a "weak moment." But forgiving others for their misdeeds, especially when it affects us in seriously adverse ways, is extremely difficult.

God doesn't have that problem. In the well-known parable of the prodigal son, Jesus tells us that the only requirements for receiving God's forgiveness are confession and repentance. The prodigal son commits a very expensive mistake, one which costs him his dignity as well as his money. The experience, though, makes him realize what a fool he has been, so he comes home, hat in hand, humbling himself before his father. His father does not do what so many of us would do. "I told you so; I hope you've finally learned your lesson," we might say. We would then proceed to administer appropriate punishment.

Divine Impact

God's response, on the other hand, is like that of the prodigal son's father, who throws a party celebrating the lost son's return. If we can believe that what Jesus is telling us is in this story is truly the way God responds to our repentance from sin, then we can then perhaps believe that God will throw a party for us when we return to Him. Imagine that—God doing something that special for you and me! That kind of response tells us that God not only forgives us, but that He moves on, forgetting the past. When we ask God to forgive us our sins and promise to try to do better, He essentially replies with something like, "What sins? I have already forgotten. You're home with me again. That's all that matters, so let's celebrate."

Further, when we accept the fact that God is really that loving toward us, we might succeed, to some degree at least, in expressing that same spirit by forgiving others their offenses against us, then throwing a party celebrating the reconciliation! When we can do that we are giving expression to that spark of divinity which lies within us.

What about the other son, though, the one who

A Father's Patience

never left, who remained loyal to the father? Here is this wastrel getting the royal treatment just because he came to his senses, while the faithful brother who never left the side of his father is seemingly ignored. The father answers the resentful son's complaint with a reminder that he could have had a party anytime he wanted to, that he always enjoyed the benefits of the father's love and generosity, while the prodigal was lost and had been found. I imagine that was little comfort to the disgruntled son.

The resentful brother had a serious attitude problem. If he truly loved his brother he would have had the same joyous response to the homecoming as his father did. Reread Matthew 5, verses 21 and 22 and see how the message there applies to the brother of the prodigal son.

Life Enrichment Axiom 18:

When we confess our sins to God and ask His forgiveness, then back it up by sincerely trying to change our ways, we can forget the past and celebrate with God at our homecoming party.

19

Future Energy Shortages Predicted
                    —CNN, July 28, 1999

An Everlasting Energy Source
God's Power Grid

In this marvelous passage from John's gospel, Jesus tells a parable in which He compares people to branches on a vine, Himself to the vine, and God the Father to the gardener. The metaphors are apt and paint a perfect picture of how God, through Christ, sustains us when we stay connected to Him. In the present age, however, agrarian references may be less meaningful than they once were, so in the commentary which follows the passage, I have used electricity to represent the power of God to sustain and energize us. The meaning of the parable of the vine is not changed, just the metaphors. The point is the same: God is the only reliable source for the power we need to lead productive lives.

Divine Impact

The Gospel of John: Chapter 15

I am the true vine, and my Father is the husbandman. Every branch in me that does not bear fruit he takes away; and every branch that does bear fruit, he prunes so that it may bring forth more fruit. Now you are clean through the word which I have spoken to you. Abide in me, and I in you. As the branch cannot bear fruit by itself unless it abides in the vine, neither can you unless you abide in me.   I am the vine, you are the branches. He that abides in me and I in him will bring forth much fruit, for without me you can do nothing. If a man does not abide in me, he is like a branch that is cut off and withers, is gathered and thrown into the fire and burned. If you abide in me, and my words abide in you, you shall ask what you will and it shall be done for you. In this way my Father is glorified, that you bear much fruit. So shall you be my disciples.

As the Father has loved me, so have I loved you. Continue in my love. If you keep my commandments you shall abide in my love, even as I have kept my Father's commandments and abide in his love. I have spoken these things to you so that my joy might remain in you and that your joy might be full. This is my commandment—that you

An Everlasting Energy Source

love one another as I have loved you. No man has any greater love than one who lays down his life for his friends. You are my friends if you do whatever I command you to do.

Divine Impact

Energy to Burn

Humankind has been ingenious in discovering a variety of energy sources in nature. Some are used as fuels to provide direct energy, others are converted to electrical power to run our homes, businesses and factories. Using everything from horsepower to atomic power, we know how to energize anything, except maybe ourselves on a lazy summer afternoon.

But none of those energy sources gives us the power to live as Jesus has commanded us to live. He gives us the commandments to use as our rules of life, and He gives us access to the means of following those rules. What this passage from the Gospel of John tells us is that if God is the source for the power we need to lead productive lives, then Jesus is the power line—the conduit of God's power. By plugging in, we receive God's power delivered to us through Jesus Christ. When we do that, we are energized for living life to the fullest, able to do all sorts of wonderful things.

Of course, we have the choice of living without power—choosing instead to live in the dark and using up our own meager self-generated energy in wasteful

An Everlasting Energy Source

pursuits. There are two ways we can lose power. One is to not plug into the source at all; the other is to allow ourselves to become victims of a power outage when the line is cut.

Choosing to not plug into a readily available source means we refuse to acknowledge our need for a power outside ourselves. If, on the other hand, we are plugged in but suffer a power outage, we must have our connection repaired if we are to continue to enjoy the benefits of a steady stream of energy. Since we all have access to the power, we simply must take the initiative to plug into it, then keep the connection in good working order. Whether we lose power by choosing to not plug in or by letting our connection fall into a state of disrepair, it is up to us to call on the power source to help us remedy the problem. If we don't, we remain in the dark.

Life Enrichment Axiom 19:

If we plug into God's power, and quickly repair any broken connection that might occur, we will always receive the power we need to live productive lives.

20

Love talked about can be easily turned aside,
but love demonstrated is irresistible.
—W. Stanley Mooneyhan

Love Is What You Do,
Not What You Feel

Jesus Gives Us the Straight Skinny on How to Love

In the introduction to this book I mentioned that some of the selected passages might singe our minds or awaken us out of our apathy or thoughtless routines. This is one of those. Here, Jesus minces no words in telling us who gets to go to heaven and who doesn't. And He doesn't mention how often we go to church, whether or not we tithe, or how much we pray or offer devotionals. His only criterion is how we treat other people.

Love Is What You Do

It all goes under the heading of obedience to the two commandments that Jesus gives us in the passage cited in Chapter 16. In this passage, He makes it clear that the two commandments are inseparable. He says that demonstrating our love for other people automatically demonstrates our love for God, because when we do, we are obeying Him.

The reverse is also true: Love God with all our hearts, souls and minds and it follows that we will love our neighbors as ourselves. When we obey these commandments we affirm our faith while making the world a better place.

Divine Impact

Matthew: Chapter 25, Verses 31 through 46

When the Son of man shall come in his glory, and all the holy angels with him, then shall he sit on the throne of his glory. And before him shall be gathered all nations, and he shall separate them one from another, as a shepherd divides his sheep from the goats. And he shall set the sheep on his right hand, but the goats on the left. Then shall the King say to them on his right hand, "Come, you blessed of my Father, inherit the kingdom prepared for you from the foundation of the world.   For I was hungry and you gave me meat. I was thirsty and you gave me drink. I was a stranger, and you took me in; naked and you clothed me. I was sick and you visited me. I was in prison and you came to me."

Then shall the righteous answer him, saying, "Lord, when did we see you hungry and feed you, or thirsty and give you drink? When did we see you as a stranger and take you in, or naked and clothe you?   Or when did we see you sick, or in prison, and come to you?   And the King shall answer and say to them, "Truly, I say to you, inasmuch as you have done it to one of the least of these my brethren, you have done it to me."

Love Is What You Do

Then shall he say to them on the left hand, "Depart from me, you cursed, into everlasting fire, prepared for the devil and his angels. For I was hungry and you gave me no meat. I was thirsty and you gave me no drink. I was a stranger and you did not take me in; naked and you did not clothe me; sick, and in prison, and you did not visit me."

Then shall they answer him, saying, "Lord, when did we see you hungry, or thirsty, or a stranger, or naked, or sick, or in prison, and did not minister unto you?"

Then shall he answer them, saying, "Truly, I say to you, inasmuch as you did not do it for one of the least of these you did not do it for me." And these shall go away into everlasting punishment, but the righteous into life eternal.

Divine Impact

Love in Action

This passage from the twenty fifth chapter of the Gospel of Matthew is one of the most troubling stories Jesus ever told. The parable of the sheep and the goats foretells our fate on judgement day: what happens to us depends on how well we have served the needs of others in this life. In this story Jesus tells us simply that only those who have served others in their times of need will share in His kingdom. For those of us who do not, the indictment is harsh.

The parable deals with fundamental human needs, but I think it is fair to assume that Jesus meant that we should address whatever serious needs people have. As times change, people's needs may change. What we see in these days of global satellite television coverage is evidence that in our world there is every conceivable kind of human suffering. The needs are many and varied.

What are we to do in the face of all this human suffering while we sit in our comfortable homes surrounded by what most of the people of the world would consider pure luxury? How far should we go in giving our time, talents and money to relieve that suffering? Is giving our fair share to the United Way good enough?   Do our tithes and offerings to our churches satisfy Jesus' requirements? And what do we do about the homeless man who stands on a street corner holding a "Will work for food" sign? We may suspect (often correctly) that he makes more money by begging than some men who work for a living. So does that suspicion relieve us of any responsibility?

Each of us must search his or her own conscience (and bank account) to find the answers to these questions. But one thing is clear. In both the parable of the sheep and goats and in the parable of the good Samaritan, Jesus says that we are indeed our brother's keeper. None of this should come as a big surprise to us, for in an earlier passage Jesus commands us to love others as we love ourselves. This serving of others, I believe, is what He means by loving our neighbors as ourselves. Moreover, in this parable, when Jesus tells us that whatever we do for our neighbor in need is the same as doing it for Him, He links the commandment to love our neighbors as ourselves to the other of His two great commandments: to love God with all our heart, soul and mind.

The parable of the sheep and the goats is a fore-telling of who goes where on judgement day. This is rough stuff and spurs me to thoroughly examine my attitudes about others in need.

Life Enrichment Axiom 20:

When we help others in need to the extent of our abilities, we are acting as God's field agents.

21

Aim at heaven and you get earth thrown in.
Aim at earth and you get neither.
> —C. S. Lewis

The Road to Paradise
Jesus Extends an Invitation

In this passage John relates Jesus' promise to His disciples that He will prepare a place for them in the place where He will be. He then extends an invitation to them to join Him there, saying that when He returns He will take them there with Him. He adds that they already know the way to get there.

When one disciple, Thomas the doubter, asks Him just how they can know the way, since they don't even know where He is going, He explains: "I am the Way." Not only that, but Jesus also says that He is the *only* way.

The way to where? We assume He means heaven. But what is heaven like, and is it worth the trip? Jesus describes it as a place of many mansions. In our imaginations we envision a large, elegant house in an exclusive neighborhood like those that may be found in most major American cities. As we read this passage we should keep in mind that Jesus was speaking to the poor and disenfranchised who had no hope of ever living in such luxury. Mansions were reserved for kings, emperors, and the very rich. Jesus knew that those ordinary people He was talking to could never have believed they would someday live in a mansion.

If Jesus were to address a crowd of Americans today with this message, how would He most likely describe heaven? In our affluent society, many Americans would not consider mansions all that special. If we were asked what heaven is like, we would probably have quite an assortment of concepts. And we might all be right, for God loves us so much that He just might provide a place that is tailor-made for our own personalities, tastes and imaginations.

The Road to Paradise

Whatever it is like, I know that it will be better than anything we can imagine. That is why this passage inspires me. It makes me realize that God's love for us is so great that He has something waiting for us that is beyond our wildest dreams.

Divine Impact

John: Chapter 14, Verses 1 through 6

Do not let your heart be troubled. You believe in God, believe also in me. In my Father's house are many mansions; if it were not so, I would have told you. I go to prepare a place for you, and if I go and prepare a place for you, I will come again and receive you unto myself, that where I am, there you may be also. And you know where I am going, and you know the way."

Thomas said to him, "Lord, we do not know where you are going, so how can we know the way?" Jesus said to him, "I am the way, the truth and the life; no man comes to the Father but by me."

The Road to Paradise

Available: Luxury Home in Exclusive Neighborhood

Once again, I quote from the writings of J. B. Phillips:

The world of creation cannot as yet see reality, not because it chooses to be blind, but because in God's purpose it has been so limited—yet it has been given hope. And the Hope is that, in the end, the whole of created life will be rescued from the tyranny of change and decay, and have its share in that magnificent liberty which can only belong to the children of God.

None of us can truly know exactly what heaven will be like, but we may be assured that it will be better than anything we can imagine. Jesus likens it to living in a mansion, which implies we will have all we could possibly want. Our wants will change, of course, and we can rely upon God to provide the maximum in true joy. But even though we cannot experience heaven until we depart this earthly life, we do get an occasional glimpse of what might be awaiting us.

I am convinced that I am in heaven already when I hear Judy Collins sing Amazing Grace, or when I hear a performance of Beethoven's Ode to Joy, or when I see one of those magnificent sunsets that God paints for us now and again, or when my grown children write me of their enduring love and of their appreciation for my love for them.

An annual highlight for me is attending a live performance of Handel's Messiah, performed by a symphony orchestra and a choir of over a hundred voices. More than once at the conclusion of the Hallelujah Chorus I have uttered the prayer, "God, my life is now complete. I can look ahead to nothing better here now, so I'm ready when you are." Of course, it didn't take me long to reassess my position. Nevertheless, at the time I was so inspired I was ready for the rapture.

While my glimpses of heaven are often centered around great music, others have different visions of life in the hereafter. My multi-handicapped son, who must avoid impact sports or risk breaking his back, believes that in heaven he will be provided a trampoline so that he can bounce to his heart's content. I encourage him in that perception because I believe that God will give him pure joy, and right now bouncing on a trampoline is my son's idea of pure joy.

I cannot possibly know what I will see or feel when I am in God's presence, but when I get glimpses of heaven on earth I think that it must be something like that, multiplied many times. Or at least the feeling will be akin to what I feel in those magical moments. Given the powerful emotions I feel at such times, I can only hope that I will be capable of taking in all of His magnificence—that He will show me how I may encompass the full measure of His goodness, His grace and His glory.

How do I know there is a God who awaits me in such a place? I read it in the Word of God, yet I recognize that it cannot be proven with a slide rule or a syllogism. I just know that it is true. Here's the way J. B. Phillips puts it:

> *This Word of God about which I believe we can be absolutely certain, and to which we can only respond through our faculty of faith, is more certain than anything else we*

know by any other of our senses. It may be illogical, it may be non-provable, it may even be nonsense to the unbeliever, but to the Christian it is not merely the confirmation of all his inklings and intuitions. It is nothing less than certainty.

Life Enrichment Axiom 21:

To get a preview of heaven, we must stop now and then to smell the roses—while remembering who made the roses.

22

Whew, that was close!
—Anonymous

It's Never Too Late
Jesus Offers Salvation to a Dying Man

Humans are very unpredictable—call us imaginative, creative, enigmatic, adventuresome, mischievous, whatever—there's not much telling what some people will do. Let's face it, we humans are often hard to understand. But one thing that is not puzzling is when someone facing death decides to start believing in God. We've all heard the old saying: "There are no atheists in foxholes." It is not literally true, of course, but there have been more than a few men on the battlefield who have prayed, even though it had not been their custom before they were threatened. Facing serious danger of most any kind will bring a person to his/her knees. And deathbed conversions are not uncommon.

In this passage from Luke's gospel, Jesus is hanging on the cross between two thieves. They are all near death. One of the thieves mocks Jesus, but the other one asks Jesus to remember him when He goes to His kingdom. Jesus' swift reply is an immediate "yes." No hesitation. No, "Well, I'll have to check the Big Rap Sheet in the Sky before I can tell you. I'll let you know." Instead, Jesus accepts the thief into the kingdom right now! Is that inspiring, or what?

It's Never Too Late

Luke: Chapter 23, Verses 39 through 42

One of the malefactors which were hanged assailed him, saying, "If you be Christ, save yourself and us." But the other one rebuked him, saying, "Don't you fear God, seeing that you are in the same condemnation? And we indeed justly, for we receive the due reward of our deeds; but this man has done nothing amiss." Then he said to Jesus, "Lord, remember me when you come into your kingdom."

And Jesus said to him, "Truly, I say to you: today you shall be with me in paradise."

How to Overcome Death, in
One Easy Lesson

In a Houston court in 1984, Karla Faye Tucker was convicted of murder and sentenced to die by lethal injection. In 1998, after years on death row in the Texas State Prison at Huntsville, the execution of Ms. Tucker was carried out. During her imprisonment she claimed to have repented of her sins and received forgiveness from God, if not from the State of Texas. In her appeal for a lesser sentence, Tucker cited her changed life as reason for leniency. Many thought she was using religious conversion as a ploy. But, who can say with certainty whether or not her conversion was real?

Perhaps anyone who believes that death is near will decide, "What have I got to lose? Just in case there is a judging God, I'd better sign on before it's too late." But I doubt that the thoughts of those facing imminent death are that flippant. More likely, I believe, that a latent need to connect with God that we are all born with is suddenly forced to the surface by the threat of spending eternity in hell.

It's Never Too Late

If God really does plant a seed of longing for Him in each of us, Jesus was probably able to discern its sudden flowering. He wouldn't have been fooled by some charlatan who was giving faith a shot just in case it turned out there really was a God.

In today's world, when someone like Karla Faye Tucker says she has repented and found God, how can anyone know if she truly has, or if she is faking it to get off death row? And even if we knew, what difference would it make? It's still the same person who committed the crime. The argument against capital punishment aside, shouldn't those who commit crimes receive the prescribed punishments, regardless of their religious convictions, old or new? Most of us would say yes, but then we think like humans. God has a different way of looking at things.

If, as Jesus tells us in the parable of the sheep and goats, we are judged in the hereafter by how we have treated others in this life, it seems clear that a murderer doesn't have much chance. But neither would a thief. The one hanging next to Jesus on Calvary might have had some good qualities, but more than likely his punishment, unlike that of Jesus, was deserved.

Divine Impact

Did Jesus care about what the man had done before? Apparently not. Jesus heard him repent and ask to be remembered in the next life. His answer to the penitent thief was something like, "Fine, you're on."

Does this mean that we have misunderstood the parable of the sheep and the goats that we read earlier? I don't think so. That parable doesn't address the question of those who do purposeful harm to others, much less the redemption of the penitent. It deals only with those who neglect others in need. Still, it is reasonable to assume that people who intentionally hurt other people would be in at least as much jeopardy of condemnation as those whose sin was neglect. But in many of His other teachings Jesus states clearly that He had come to die for the sins of the whole world. And in the parable of the prodigal son He tells us that God quickly forgives and forgets the sins of one who repents of his/her sins and comes home to God. I don't recall His mentioning a time limit.

While life is precious and we can sympathize with one who is facing death, the loss of life in this world is secondary to the issue of where a soul will spend eternity. God knows if Karla Faye Tucker was sincere in her repentance, and I am certain that He will deal with her and with all the rest of us mercifully, applying His superior form of justice.

God is the father of us all. I am convinced that He always has the welcome mat out for us, even until our dying breath.

Life Enrichment Axiom 22:

We save ourselves a lot of grief if we come early to God's party, but it is better to come late than not at all.

23

Life is an adventure directed by God.
—Paul Tournier

Not to Worry

The Apostle Paul Says It Will All Work Out

This passage from Paul's letter to the Romans is key to understanding God's relationship to people who love Him. And on the surface it contradicts one of the statements I made in the introduction to the story of Adam and Eve in Chapter 2 of this book. In discussing why I thought free will was necessary for anything to have value, I stated that God would not have made us a "bunch of robots while He sat in heaven acting as a main-frame computer controlling our every action." We were preparing to read the story of the Fall, the first time humans realized they had free will. In that story, Adam and Eve disobeyed God, alienating themselves from Him. Thus was launched human history, formed by the collective and interacting choices of generation after generation of men and women. Now the Apostle Paul comes along and writes his letter to the Romans, in which he includes in Chapter 8 this verse which implies that God may indeed be controlling things from on high. As you read this verse, see how you can reconcile human free will with Paul's claim.

Divine Impact

Romans Chapter 8, Verse 28

And we know that all things work together for good for those who love God, to those who are called according to his purpose.

Not to Worry

Don't Worry, Be Happy

The title of this commentary comes from a popular song of the 1980's. I do not know what was in the mind of the composer of these lyrics, nor can I be absolutely certain what Paul meant by this verse from his letter to the Romans: *For we know that all things work together for good for those who love God, who are called according to His purpose.* What I believe Paul meant was that if we love God we can stop worrying and be happy, just like the 1980's popular song says. But how does Paul's assertion jibe with human free will? If all things are going to work out for good, how can anyone's choices to do wrong things have any weight? Is God really controlling the whole show and is our so-called free will just an illusion to us uninformed puppets?

The answer, I believe, is that God indeed gives us free will for the reasons covered in Chapter 2. But I also believe that He has a master plan, and that He loves us enough to stay involved in human history. One thing many of us forget all too often is that God is too big for our small minds: that He is omnipotent, omniscient, and omnipresent, and that He exists outside our space-time continuum. If we can accept those premises, and recognize that God can at once see all of human history from start to finish or from finish to start as He chooses, why could He not intervene in order to have everything fit His master plan—not by forcing us to change our choices, but by providing those who love Him with the grace to make the choices that advance His plan?

The last phrase in the verse reveals an important condition: "...(for those) who are called according to His purpose." This suggests that Paul believed that God gives His children what we essentially ask Him for when we make our commitments to Him—guidance to do things His way. When we accept God's guidance, I believe Paul is saying, then we become willing, if unwitting, instruments of His plan.

In the passage immediately preceding this verse, Paul assured his readers that God sends His Spirit to provide help for believers when they need it. The 28th verse then is a logical extension of that assurance, i.e., that if God's Spirit is at work in the situation, then things will, *of course*, work out to the proper conclusion, even though the recipients of God's grace via His Spirit may not be aware (at least at the time) of how any good can come out of the situation. The way I see it, Paul's assertion that all things will work out for good might be said today like this: "Relax, God's got things under control, so you needn't be concerned with the outcome." In other words, "Don't Worry, Be Happy."

The first time I thoughtfully read this verse I did not understand how it could possibly be true. I reasoned that, if this is true, then why do those who love God have troubles like everyone else? I read other versions of the Bible to see if the meaning of the verse in my translation was perhaps a little off. But no, what Paul wrote is clear: "all things work together for good for those who love God and are called according to His purpose." I believe I qualify as one who loves God, but it took me years of observing the outcomes of what had started as some sort of trouble to realize that Paul had it right, although I often wondered *how long* it would take God to work things out for good.

Notice the verse does not say *when* we will know

that things work together for good. During the time I was assessing the applicability of Paul's statement to my own experience, I learned that often the "trouble" in question may take a long, twisted road that only an omniscient God can follow before it is resolved—before we mortals can see why it all happened in the first place.

In Chapter 7 of this book about an Old Testament Proverb, I cited one example from my own life—the birth of my multi-handicapped son—of how I learned, albeit very slowly, to trust God with my problems. This verse from Paul's letter to the Romans contains the same lesson as does the proverb, but instead of merely providing advice, Paul explains that when we trust God with a situation or problem, we can then forget about it and go on living joyously.

When my son was born with all those "troubles" I mentioned in Chapter 7, I was furious with God. But now, knowing what a fine young man he has turned out to be, I know that God did indeed work out things for good, and in more ways than one, as is usually the case when God has His way. As my son endured multiple surgical procedures, his mother and I gained maturity, resilience and compassion, not only for our son, but also for the other handicapped children we encountered. And who knows what might have happened if our son had been "normal." Drug addiction? Killed or maimed in a car accident or in war? God may have blessed him and us more than we know.

Another application of the lesson found in this passage is my being drafted into the Army when I had a wife and two small children to support. It was peacetime, so there was no threat of being sent into combat. Nevertheless, I wanted to avoid service.

Leaving my job to go off to serve in the Army, with its attendant financial loss, was no more than an inconvenience, but to my self-centered, immature mind, it was ruinous. I made a big deal out of it and argued with the draft board, but to no avail. I was sent off to do my two years of duty. During the trip to the base where I was to do basic training, I tried to figure out a way to get out of serving. I even prayed to God for help.

Fortunately, God said no to my request, and did for me what I did not have the sense or courage to do for myself. A couple of months into military service and I

Divine Impact

begrudgingly admitted that I didn't mind it too much. After six months, I was assigned choice duty, which I re-enlisted to get, and was actually enjoying the Army. When I was discharged after almost three and a half years, I realized that I was a more mature, physically fit man than I had been. And, wonder of wonders, my wife and children did not go hungry. I thanked God that He did it His way and not mine.

The people of the Old Testament, I think, took as a given the principle of God's total control over all of life. One good example is found in the story of Joseph (yes, the same Joseph who had that marvelous Technicolor dreamcoat). As a youth, Joseph was sold by his brothers to a caravan of traveling salesmen, who wound up selling him to the Pharaoh in Egypt. After a while, Joseph found favor with Pharaoh and was given a position of authority in Egypt. Years later, his brothers, desperate for food to keep themselves and their father, Jacob, alive, came calling on Joseph for help, not realizing it was him. They did not recognize their now grown-up little brother. He recognized them but kept it to himself. After he played a few tricks on them he finally got them together for a dinner party,

Not to Worry

and, amidst re-union tears, he confessed to them who he was. And right then and there Joseph knew that God had done all this for a purpose. He told his brothers, "God has sent me before you to preserve a remnant on earth, and to keep alive for you many survivors. So it was not you who sent me, but God." Clearly, Joseph was well-connected to God, so he could see how he was part of God's plan.

After Joseph took care of his brothers' needs, he then had them bring their father to Egypt. Soon the whole family was reunited, had plenty to eat, and were given new fertile land to settle. So all things did work out for good.

But that's not the end of the story. Years later, under a new pharaoh, the descendants of Joseph's family were driven into slavery, setting up the much later exodus of the Jews from Egypt under the leadership of a fellow named Moses. And, as they say, the rest is history. In fact, when Joseph's brothers sold him to the traveling salesmen, they initiated a chain of events that led to the Jewish settlement of the Promised Land and all the history of the Jewish people which followed. Apparently, from the very first it was

Divine Impact

all part of God's plan. God had put them there to gain in numbers and to prepare for becoming a new nation. So, today when we read of the continuing saga of Israel, let us keep in mind that whatever happens might also be part of God's plan and just might work out for good.

It is hard for us to see how any good can come from the never-ending conflict in the Holy Land, but God is a lot more patient than we are. Had Joseph known that his descendants would be cast into slavery, he probably would not have asked his father and his brothers to stay in Egypt. But he was part of God's plan. I do not mean to imply that God causes us to do wrong things or to do things which might lead to trouble just so He can show us how clever He is in working things out. But knowing that we will make stupid mistakes, He stands ready to take the lemons we produce and make lemonade out of them. He then adds the lemonade to the banquet of human history.

Clearly, God's work is too complicated for our relatively small minds to completely comprehend. What I see in the story of Joseph and many other Old Testament stories is God's hand at work on a grand

scale. What I see in my own experience is God working on a much smaller scale, but work which nevertheless somehow fits into the big picture. Together,
these observations assure me that Paul was right
when he wrote that "all things work together for good
for those who love God."

Life Enrichment Axiom 23:

*When we let go of our worries and trust
God to work things out for good, we are
freed to live the joyous lives He meant us to
live.*

24

Love is the only sane and satisfactory answer
to the problem of human existence.
—Erich Fromm

Love Is Everything

The Apostle Paul's Treatise on Love

The thirteenth chapter of Paul's First Letter to the Corinthians is often called the "love chapter." In it Paul describes real love, sacrificial love—the kind that is backed up with action. When you read this passage, compare Paul's definition of love to what is more commonly perceived as love in today's society.

Perhaps Paul considered it necessary to explain this God-like kind of love to the new Christians in Corinth precisely because it was so alien to them. A personal God who loved humankind in the way Paul described

187

Love Is Everything

was a totally revolutionary concept of an object of worship. The pagan gods within their experience had no such attributes. And for the people in Corinth to love with that same selfless focus on the beloved probably seemed like a lofty, absurd ideal.

Today many of us probably regard sacrificial love the same way. After all, in our daily contacts with others and our exposures to the media, we are surrounded by reminders of how much we are to get out of life, not how much we are to give.

I am inspired by this passage for two reasons: one, it details for me the kind of love God has for me and for all of us; and, two, it spells out for me the sort of attitude I must develop in my relationships with other people.

Divine Impact

Paul's First Letter to the Corinthians: Chapter 13

Though I speak with the tongues of men and of angels, and have not love, I am like clanging brass or a tinkling cymbal.

And though I have the gift of prophecy and understand all mysteries and all knowledge; and though I have all faith so that I could remove mountains, and have not love, I am nothing. And though I give away all I have to feed the poor, and though I give my body to be burned, and have not love, I gain nothing.

Love is longsuffering and is kind. Love does not envy; love does not boast, is not puffed up, does not behave in an unseemly manner, does not seek attention, is not easily provoked, and thinks no evil. It does not rejoice in iniquity, but rejoices in the truth. Love bears all things, believes all things, hopes all things, endures all things.

Love never fails. But if there are prophecies, they shall fail; if there are tongues, they shall cease; if there is knowledge, it shall vanish away. For we know in part and we prophesy in part. But when that which is perfect comes, then that which is in part shall be done away.

Love Is Everything

When I was a child, I spoke as a child, I understood as a child, I thought as a child. But when I became a man I put away childish things. For now we see through a glass darkly, but then face to face. Now I know in part, but then shall I know, just as I am known.   And now abides faith, hope, love—these three; but the greatest of these is love.

Divine Impact

A Whole Lotta Lovin' Goin' On

Here are four typical scenarios in modern human experience:

A man attempts to seduce a woman, telling her that he loves her.

A teenager sees a new CD by the hottest new band and buys it for his or her best friend.

Parents on a limited income do without life's amenities so their child may attend college.

Two women, while shopping, spot a new dress and one exclaims, "I love this, don't you?"

Sounds like a whole lot of loving, doesn't it? But are these all expressions of true love? It is obvious that the feelings and thoughts they represent are different in certain ways, but are they all genuine love? The English language suffers for having just one word to represent all these different emotions. First century Greek, which Paul used in his letter to the Corinthians, had four separate words to represent the emotions we now lump together as love.

Love Is Everything

The word *love* in Paul's letter is inadequately translated from the Greek word *agape*. *Agape* is a particular kind of love, perhaps best defined as self-sacrificing love, the kind of love God has for us. The King James version uses the word "charity" for *agape*, but that is not adequate for today's reader either, although what we think of as charity is probably close to what the Greeks meant as *agape*.

So, let us think of love in Paul's letter as "sacrificial love." We humans are capable of that kind of love, but, of course, to a far lesser degree than is God. It is the kind of love good parents have for their children, and the kind heroes who risk their own lives have for those they rescue, even if they do not know them. This is the kind of love Jesus talks about when He says love God and love your neighbor. It is the kind that is at work when we provide for the needs of others, as Jesus talks about in the parable of the sheep and the goats.

Today we often think of love as a *feeling* we have for someone. Warm fuzzy feelings are fine, but they are of little value unless they are expressed in action. I don't really love my wife if I ignore her needs or cheat on her. I can tell her three times a day how much I love her, but if I never show it by doing what is in her best interests, rather than in my own, then I'm not really loving her.

Agape, the God-like, sacrificial love Paul claimed as being superior to hope and faith, requires much from us. This passage bears re-reading over and over again until we truly realize what this kind of love involves. But imagine what the world would be like if we all expressed the *agape* kind of love, not only for our spouses, our children and other family members, but also for each person we encounter. We wouldn't recognize the place.

Life Enrichment Axiom 24:

When we open ourselves to God's love for us, He will enable us to emulate His love in our relationships with others.

25

Are You Ready for War?
The Battle With Evil is Underway

Paul wrote his letter to the Christians at Ephesus from his prison cell in Rome. More than likely, he saw Roman soldiers while there, and had no doubt seen many of them in occupied Palestine and in his travels across much of the Empire. The sight of armed and armored Roman soldiers must have inspired him to conclude his letter with an exhortation to his readers to put on a special kind of armor as protection against the forces of evil. It is a metaphor that could be easily understood by the people of the Roman Empire in the first century.

Divine Impact

Twenty centuries later the forces of evil have not yet been subdued. They are ever with us, and it seems that periodically they bring in fresh troops to renew their attacks on people. So it behooves us today to use all the protection we can get to withstand the enemy's onslaughts. Paul tells us what equipment we need.

Are You Ready for War?

Paul's Letter to the Ephesians:
Chapter 6, Verses 10 through 17

Finally, my brethren, be strong in the Lord and in the power of his might. Put on the whole armor of God so that you may be able to stand against the wiles of the devil. For we wrestle not against flesh and blood, but against principalities, against powers, against the rulers of the darkness of this world, against spiritual wickedness in high places.

So, take up the whole armor of God so that you may be able to withstand the evil day, and having done all, to stand. Stand and gird your loins with truth, wearing the breastplate of righteousness and with your feet shod with the preparation of the gospel of peace. Above all, take the shield of faith, with which you shall be able to quench all the fiery darts of the wicked. And take the helmet of salvation and the sword of the Spirit, which is the word of God, praying always with all prayer and supplication in the Spirit, and watching with all perseverance and supplication for all saints.

Divine Impact

It's All Out War

In the late 1970's, comedian Flip Wilson had a weekly television show in which he played a female character named Geraldine. When anyone discovered that Geraldine had done something wrong, she blamed it on the devil. The line, "The devil made me do it," always got a laugh, and even entered the public vernacular for a time. As I recall this comedic treatment of Satan, I see in my mind's eye the cartoonish creature in red tights we are all familiar with. He has an impish grin, horns sprouting from his head and a tail protruding from his rear. He carries a pitchfork, too, presumably to pitch sinners into the eternal flames of hell.

We've all seen this caricature of the devil, often sitting on a conflicted person's shoulder, while the little demon's angelic opposite is perched on the person's other shoulder. The two miniature spirits whisper advice to their "client," who has to choose between good and evil based on the counsel of these two representatives from hell and heaven, respectively. While this simple representation of the personification of good and evil might evoke a chuckle, to my way of thinking it is not all that far from the truth. It is a humorous, bloodless myth that points to the truth that there is in fact a battle between good and evil going on. And you and I are the prizes being fought over.

The existence of Satan is an issue that has been roundly debated, even among some believers. He is called by many names—the devil, the Evil One, Lucifer, Old Nick, Beelzebul, and the Prince of Darkness, to name some of the more familiar ones. Whatever we call him, he is the personification of evil, the antithesis of God, and the enemy of all who side with God in the struggle of good versus evil. He, or it, is spirit and therefore cannot be seen. Nor can his existence be proven. But the effects of his work certainly can be seen, just as the effects of gravity and wind can be seen, while the forces themselves cannot be. Clearly evil exists, whether or not we personify it with a name like Satan or any of the other labels we have given this spirit. God is spirit, too, and the battle for our souls is fought constantly between our Creator and the evil one who wishes to steal us from Him. It is nothing short of war.

The spiritual war that has been raging since Adam and Eve first tasted freedom of choice is not being fought according to the Geneva Convention or any other set of rules. Satan is not an honorable adversary, but a terrorist of the worst kind. He is ready, willing and able to do anything he can to keep us out of God's camp. He is devious, conniving, deceitful, and treacherous. He hits below the belt, stabs in the back, and often works in disguise. He is a rat, a sneak, a spy, an imposter, a snake in the grass, and a wolf in sheep's clothing. He is a con artist, a schemer, and a traitor. He is Judas and Benedict Arnold. He makes Hitler and Osama bin Laden look like saints. Do I think he's bad? He's all those things and worse.

We tend to think of Satan when we witness terrible things being done by people who seem to care nothing for the lives of others, whatever their ostensible motives might be. Murder, rape, terrorist attacks, and other heinous crimes are logically considered the work of Satan. But Satan may not care as much about those things as we do, as they often tend to stir us to a stronger resolve to eradicate evil. I imagine that the evil one isn't too interested in the deaths of innocent people, except in the sense that he realizes he had missed his opportunity to subvert them to his way.

Are You Ready for War?

When they are dead, it's too late. He might delight, however, in the death of a person possessed of evil, who because of his demise is then safely ensconced in hell and no longer in danger of being swept away from his death bed by God. So, I suppose he rejoices at the deaths of those whom he has won over in this life, and is disappointed when a godly person dies and is then removed from his list of prospects.

Experience suggests that Satan often disguises himself as our friend, one interested in letting us have a good time, or making us feel good about what we have accomplished. (Pride seems to be one of his favorite sins.) And he's not too big on the large, cataclysmic evils, as he cannot be too certain of their effects on our souls. Instead he likes to whittle away at our unsuspecting and vulnerable virtues. He is very patient. A clever, and I believe accurate, depiction of how Satan must think and work may be found in C. S. Lewis' classic work, *The Screwtape Letters*. The book is comprised of a series of letters written by an assistant devil named Screwtape, who refers to his boss, Satan, as "Our Father Below."

The recipient of the letters is Screwtape's nephew,

Divine Impact

Wormwood, who is on assignment on Earth during the early years of World War II. The following brief excerpt from one of the letters expresses the attitudes of underworld spirits. Wormwood has just advised his uncle Screwtape that the Germans were about to begin bombing the town in England where his human target lives. Screwtape's response includes this advice:

> *The tension of human nerves during noise, danger, and fatigue makes them prone to any violent emotion and it is only a question of guiding this susceptibility into the right channels. If conscience resists, muddle him. Let him say that he feels hatred not on his own behalf but on that of the women and children, and that a Christian is told to forgive his own, not other people's enemies. In other words let him consider himself sufficiently identified with the women and children to feel hatred on their behalf, but not sufficiently identified to regard their enemies as his own and therefore proper objects of forgiveness.*

Are You Ready for War?

But Hatred is best combined with Fear. Cowardice, alone of all the vices, is purely painful—horrible to anticipate, horrible to feel, horrible to remember; Hatred has its pleasures. It is therefore often the compensation by which a frightened man reimburses himself for the miseries of Fear. The more he fears, the more he will hate. And Hatred is also a good anodyne for shame. To make a deep wound in his charity, you should therefore first defeat his courage.

So, Geraldine probably had it right. The devil did make her do it.

Clearly, we must protect ourselves against any force which connives to make us spend eternity in pain and sorrow. And in the sixth chapter of Paul's letter to the Ephesians we learn how to do that: We must equip ourselves with truth, right behavior, faith, salvation, the gospel of peace, the Holy Spirit who works through the Word of God, and prayer for ourselves and for others. So equipped, we are ready for the onslaughts of the evil one.

Life Enrichment Axiom 25:

When we choose God's side in the war between good and evil, God supplies the means to keep the enemy from getting to us.

Living An Enriched Life

Don't Try This Alone

We have just navigated all 25 chapters—25 passages from the Bible and how I believe they can enrich your life as they have mine. But I must add this warning: Do not try to incorporate the 25 life enrichment axioms, which conclude the chapters, into your rules of life without getting some help. That might be dangerous to your spiritual health.

What? Isn't that the purpose of the book—to use these simple axioms as guides to living enriched lives? The answer is a definite yes, but think back and remember that throughout the book I have encouraged readers to stay connected to God. The suggestions on how to live enriched lives as stated in the axioms are less than worthless if God is not involved in the process of applying them. To do that, He must become the center of our lives. That is why I made that assertion the core of Life Enrichment Axiom 1 at the conclusion of Chapter 1, as it is the foundation of all the other axioms. God created us and His grace sustains us. Any attempt on our part to go it alone can only end tragically.

It is our natural tendency to want to be self-reliant, especially in America, a nation built on self-reliance. But being self-reliant spiritually is a whole lot different from gathering up the courage to strike out on a new worldly adventure. I happen to believe that God admires that kind of courage, and expects it of us when the need exists. A strong, bold leader is essential to the achievement of important goals that allow for progress. God didn't design us to be wimps.

In contrast, spiritual self-reliance achieves nothing, but only gets us into trouble. It's what got things off on the wrong foot in the Garden of Eden. Remember that Adam and Eve initiated our alienation from God by trying to be gods themselves. All they really wanted to do was make their own rules for living. May we not repeat their gross error!

Hopefully, we have learned a lesson from Adam and Eve. We have enough problems living with the results of what they started without emulating them. The fact is they couldn't get things right by going it alone, and neither can we. We need some Big Time help. To get it, humility before God is required.

I have learned this lesson the hard way—from personal experience. I have made plenty of mistakes, some of them quite serious. By trying to do things my way and not seeking God's guidance, I have caused myself, my family and others much unnecessary trouble. Perhaps my own difficult and continuing learning process, and the important role Bible reading has had in it, is the reason why I am so convinced that the Bible gives us vital access to God's messages for us. I have learned much from Him through His Holy Word, and it has enriched my life more than I can communicate. My only regret is that I didn't look for God's help through the Scriptures a lot sooner than I did.

Reading the Bible is just one of the ways we stay connected to God. Prayer is another critical protective device. Keeping the line of communication with God open requires more than occasional contact. It takes constant, genuine, open communication. The last line in the last selected Bible passage in this Book, taken from the 18th verse of the sixth chapter of Ephesians, contains Paul's admonishment that we "pray always." This regular communion helps us keep God at the center of our lives. Praying all day every day in every situation is a habit that forms slowly, and with our proclivity for self-indulgence, it is a habit which will probably never be fully developed. Still, it is something we should work at, and with God's help, we will succeed to the degree our humanness allows.

Regular Bible reading, unceasing prayer, and applying the Life Enrichment Axioms are all guides on the road toward spiritual maturity, the attainment of which is, in the end, our best defense against the wiles of Satan. But it is a never ending journey that we undertake. As of today, I have no idea how much I have yet to learn. I know it is much, and, with God as my navigator, I look forward with great anticipation to the adventure that lies ahead. I invite you to join me.

Life Enrichment Axioms

1. When we realize the awesome power of God as expressed in His creation, we have taken the first step in allowing Him to reside in the core of our being. And with Him as our center, we are open to His desire to enrich our lives.

2. Recognizing that God gave us freedom of choice to establish our value system, we know that by choosing to seek God's guidance we will make better, life-enriching decisions.

3. We are ready to enter into an important relationship only when we are willing to make a commitment to give it our all and stay the course.

4. Loyalty means sticking by those to whom we have made commitments, and not switching sides when it seems to be of more advantage to us. In this way we will earn the trust and respect of others.

5. When we work at developing a strong faith in God, our character will strengthen and our self-esteem will grow.

Life Enrichment Axioms

6. Keeping the Bible near us wherever we are gives us instant access to words of comfort and encouragement.

7. Trusting God means being patient and waiting to see how, in His wisdom, He works things out.

8. With a strong vision of where we want to be in the future, as individuals, as families, and as a nation, and with God as our guide, we will continue, to enjoy life, liberty and the pursuit of happiness.

9. When we practice the virtue of hope we open ourselves to life's abundance, both in the present world and in the one beyond.

10. Whether we are rich or poor, a leader or a follower, if we recognize that we all need God and earnestly seek Him out, He will be there for us.

11. Let the mysteries of God remind us that He is beyond our understanding and that we are simply to trust Him to do what is best in the long run.

Life Enrichment Axioms

12. If we think of prayer as the tuner in our built-in radio, we can find God's frequency, tune out the static of worldly distractions, and hear God's message of joy, peace, hope and love.

13. When we become weighed down by the troubles of this world, let us take heart by remembering that God will balance the scales later.

14. While we cannot always control the thoughts that enter our heads, by asking God to remove the ones that do not glorify Him, He will, in time, show us how to control the tendencies.

15. By worshiping God and not material possessions, we will gain the necessary wisdom to handle our finances in ways which provide for ourselves, our families and the needs of others.

16. Simplifying our lives to the extent we can allows us to focus more on our relationships with God, family and neighbor.

Life Enrichment Axioms

17. When we turn our troubles over to God we are freed from despair and discontent.

18. When we confess our sins to God and ask His forgiveness, then sincerely try to change our ways, we can forget the past and celebrate with God at our homecoming party.

19. If we plug into God's power, and quickly repair any broken connection that might occur, we will always receive the power we need to lead productive lives.

20. When we help others in need to the extent of our abilities, we are acting as God's field agents.

21. To get a preview of heaven, we must stop now and then to smell the roses—while remembering who made the roses.

22. We save ourselves a lot of grief if we come to God's party early, but it is better to come late than not at all.

Life Enrichment Axioms

23. When we let go of our worries and trust God to work things out for good, we are freed to live the joyous lives He meant us to live.

24. When we open ourselves to God's love for us, He will enable us to emulate His love in our relationships with others.

25. When we choose God's side in the war between good and evil, God supplies the means to keep the enemy from getting to us.

The Bible is the *book of adventure
and must be read as such.*
—Paul Tournier

CPSIA information can be obtained
at www.ICGtesting.com
Printed in the USA
FSOW02n0928210315
5804FS